T0330554

'Collating the "state of the art" for a diverse field like OM, that has always combined a wide range of social science and engineering scholarship, is a really challenging task. This engaging book succeeds by adopting a novel perspective inspired by the process of curation in the visual arts. The reader is engaged in detailed discussion of the past, present, and potential future of OM research though a series of chapters, each framed by analogous reflections on some extraordinary artistic masterpieces.'

—Professor Matthias Holweg, American Standard
Companies Professor of Operations Management,
Saïd Business School, University of Oxford, UK

'Regardless of whether you are new PhD student or experienced faculty member, or just someone who wants to get to grips with where the field of Operations Management "is at", I strongly recommend you read Michael Lewis' new text as it paints a stimulating picture of the "state of the art".'

— Professor Andy Neely, Pro-Vice-Chancellor
for Enterprise and Business Relations,
University of Cambridge, UK

Operations Management

Operations Management (OM) is a multi-faceted blend of myriad academic and practical disciplines – from engineering and economics via mathematics and marketing, to systems and psychology. To capture the state of the art, the book reviews contemporary and classic scholarship in one of the oldest business and management disciplines. To offer the reader a thought-provoking point of entry into the selected sources, the book curates its content as an imaginary exhibit, each chapter a thematic OM 'gallery' (process; planning and control; people; strategy and measurement; technology) introduced by a description of some extraordinary artefacts, paintings, sculptures and architecture.

The content has been curated around three principles intended to benefit the casual reader and both new and established OM scholars. First, it incorporates works that build on, or help to distinguish, fundamental tenets from more transitory fads. Second, the text makes significant efforts to try and balance the gravitational pull of the factory, (even though this may not offer an accurate representation of the majority of the field) and third, to try to keep managerial rather than technical/analytical concerns to the fore.

This concise book provides a useful overview of current and classic OM research. Written by a leading authority, it is intended to be a valuable and engaging resource for both students and scholars of business.

Michael A. Lewis is Professor of Operations and Supply Management at the University of Bath. He is the author of numerous articles and books.

State of the Art in Business Research
Series Editor: Geoffrey Wood

Recent advances in theory, methods and applied knowledge (alongside structural changes in the global economic ecosystem) have presented researchers with challenges in seeking to stay abreast of their fields and navigate new scholarly terrains.

State of the Art in Business Research presents shortform books which provide an expert map to guide readers through new and rapidly evolving areas of research. Each title will provide an overview of the area, a guide to the key literature and theories and time-saving summaries of how theory interacts with practice.

As a collection, these books provide a library of theoretical and conceptual insights, and exposure to novel research tools and applied knowledge, that aid and facilitate in defining the state of the art, as a foundation stone for a new generation of research.

Network Industries
A Research Overview
Matthias Finger

Strategic Risk Management
A Research Overview
Torben Juul Andersen & Johanna Sax

Management and Organizational History
A Research Overview
Albert J. Mills & Milorad M. Novicevic

Employee Engagement
A Research Overview
Brad Shuck

Operations Management
A Research Overview
Michael A. Lewis

For more information about this series, please visit: www.routledge.com/State-of-the-Art-in-Business-Research/book-series/START

Operations Management

A Research Overview

Michael A. Lewis

Routledge
Taylor & Francis Group

LONDON AND NEW YORK

First published 2020
by Routledge
2 Park Square, Milton Park, Abingdon, Oxon OX14 4RN

and by Routledge
52 Vanderbilt Avenue, New York, NY 10017

Routledge is an imprint of the Taylor & Francis Group, an informa business

British Library Cataloguing-in-Publication Data
A catalogue record for this book is available from the British Library

Library of Congress Cataloging-in-Publication Data
A catalog record for this book has been requested

ISBN: 978-1-138-49062-8 (hbk)
ISBN: 978-1-351-03498-2 (ebk)

Typeset in Times New Roman
by Apex CoVantage, LLC

For Owen Arthur and Dylan Henry Lewis, as promised

Contents

Foreword

Each of the following chapters is introduced, perhaps framed is a better term, by some analogous, and hopefully engaging, reflections on a series of extraordinary pieces of art; paintings, sculptures, architecture, collages, etc. These discussions sometimes touch on the subject of the artwork, sometimes when it was produced, sometimes how it was produced and sometimes the underlying conceptual intent. Unfortunately, no actual images of the artworks are included and so, in addition to your imagination, I strongly encourage you seek them out.

MAL
August 2019

1 Introduction

Curating a state of the OM art?

The notion of a singular *state of the art*[1] in Operations Management (OM) is problematic. The field is a rich blend of myriad academic and practical disciplines – from engineering and economics via mathematics and marketing, to systems and psychology and beyond. Consequently, a better description of what this book sets out to achieve emerges from a more literal reading of the word 'art': the expression of human creative skill and imagination in the production of, typically, visual and aesthetically pleasing artefacts. Although the art world might seem far removed from OM's (social) scientific motivations and goals,[2] it is the process of curation – selecting, interpreting and presenting important artworks – that proved inspirational. Think therefore of what follows as a scholarly OM exhibit.

It is not intended to be comprehensive – indeed the editorial structure of the Routledge series means that although OM has been profoundly influenced by a supply chain 'turn', this material is not really addressed – but the final themes were chosen to address the breadth of contemporary OM scholarship whilst also allowing the reader to connect to its (extended) heritage.[3] Stretching this metaphor, and to help engage and motivate the reader, each chapter is introduced by a 'gallery' presenting, albeit in the readers' imagination, a series of relevant artworks.

The beginnings of OM

Our introductory, imaginary, OM gallery presents a triptych of artefacts. The first is a small piece of shaped black flint, a paleolithic hand axe. The 'Happisburgh hand axe' was found by a dog-walker on a Norfolk beach in 2000 and is the oldest (circa 550,000 BC, pre-Neanderthal) found in northwest Europe. Such a tool would have had a variety of uses, the carefully (re)sharpened edge could be used for scraping, chopping and butchering (mammoth butchery sites have been found in the same area) while the blunt end could have been used as a mallet. Interestingly, it has clearly been shaped more carefully and completely than needed for functional purposes, suggesting someone wanted to create a tool that was both good to use and aesthetically pleasing. This beautiful and practical ancient object reminds us that the use of specialized tools is as old as humanity itself and that many seemingly contemporary operational challenges are entwined with our most basic human characteristics. Archaeologists who study the very earliest societies around the world have found extensive evidence of different techniques for making points, blades, scrapers and cutters, suggesting the existence of specialist toolmakers and, consequently, the division of labour that requires organized collaborative social structures. Consider the idea of human universals, first proposed by celebrated anthropologist Donald Brown, to describe "those features of culture, society, language, behavior, and psyche for which there are no known exception". His list of universals included key foundational concepts for OM such as tools and tool making (and tools to make tools), division of labour, cooperation, cooperative labour, cyclicity of time, etc.

Flanking the stone axe are two life-sized armoured warrior figures from the first Emperor of China, Qin Shi Huang's, Terracotta Army (pre-210 BC). One is a kneeling archer in full armour (even the stitches on his sole are visible) and the other a General dressed to show status and identity. More than 8,000 soldiers (plus 130 chariots with 520 horses, 150 cavalry horses, etc.) have been found in Shaanxi province and it is believed that the production of such an extraordinary range of fully realized and detailed warrior and chariot sculptures was probably organized using, what would today be recognized as, some form of cellular manufacturing, with various multi-skilled units exploiting significant levels of product standardization (i.e., 10 different faces, various uniforms, some wearing shin pads, some long or short trousers, some padded; and body armours varying depending on rank, function, etc.: Martinón-Torres et al. 2014).

Finally, hanging on the wall there is Canaletto's (1732) painting of the entrance to the Venice Arsenale.[4] Canaletto or Giovanni Antonio Canal (1697–1768) was a celebrated Italian painter of city views whose works are notable for their accuracy. He normally painted 'in the field' and consequently his pictures are full of atmospheric effects and authentic local colours (this has led some to assert his work could be seen as having anticipated Impressionism). The Arsenale complex built in 1104, located approximately a fifteen-minute walk from St. Mark's Square, was arguably the greatest manufactory[5] of the pre-industrial world, eventually covering an area of 115 acres, surrounded by 2.5 miles of brick walls (30ft high in places), with berths for 80 galleys (plus dry docks and a foundry). At its peak productive capacity in the 15th and 16th centuries, more than 4000 employees (Arsenalotti) – including gunmakers, oarmakers, mastmakers and sailmakers – passed every day through this entrance to work in the Factory of Marvels,[6] *L'Officina delle Meraviglie*. It could prepare 30 galleys for sea in 10 days (Lane 1934, 1973). It was a vertically integrated operation with hulls, and other standard parts, batch manufactured and stored as inventory. These parts could then be assembled into a finished product in a matter of hours, as and when required – using canals as conveyors to move ships to the workers. Such a complex system also required the growth of new managerial concepts such as cost accounting (Zan 2004) and the idea of work in progress (WIP). The Arsenale finally closed as a production site in 1810, unable to adapt to the more innovative 18th-century shipbuilding that emerged during the period that is now known as the Industrial Revolution. Today, although much of the Arsenale site is still in use by the Italian

Navy it has also, since 1999, been home to some of the Venice Art Biennale – a celebrated contemporary visual art exhibition held (unsurprisingly) biennially in odd-numbered years. Many national pavilions – including Italy, China and various African, Asian and South American countries – are located here. Most of these ancient industrial buildings have only been partially restored, creating a wonderful visual contrast with the contemporary artworks on show.

These artefacts serve to highlight the many perspectives and alternate narratives to be considered when detailing the emergence of contemporary OM. Indeed, as the Terracotta Army (or the Pyramids, or the Arsenale, or the Spanish Royal Tobacco factory (Carmona et al. 1997), etc.) reveal, much of what was 'discovered' may have already long been known (cf. Voss 2007). Nonetheless it is the dramatic 18th-century events that initially took place in the British textile industry (Berg 1994; Landes 1999) that are most closely linked with the articulation and application of key tenets of what would become the OM field. In 1781, Britain consumed 5 million pounds of raw cotton; by 1818, 164 million; by 1850, 588 million. By the late 19th century, England had become the most highly industrialized country that had ever been seen.

The Industrial Revolution is often presented as if it were all about engineering, a series of technological innovations, such as James Watt's separate condenser steam engine or John Kay's 'flying shuttle' for weaving (patented in 1733) or James Hargreaves' 'spinning jenny' (patented in 1764, by the time of his death in 1778, there were around 20,000 spinning jennys across the UK) which solved the efficiency imbalance between spinning and weaving or Samuel Crompton's Spinning Mule (invented but not patented – he was too poor – in 1775) or Eli Whitney's cotton engine, gin for short (1794), etc. Similarly, Marc Isambard Brunel (the French-born father of Isambard Kingdom Brunel) completed his block-making machines for the Portsmouth Naval dockyard (Gilbert 1965; Cooper 1981) in 1808. They were the first to use machine tools to make equipment (rigging blocks) with interchangeable parts and saved the Admiralty many thousands of pounds, allowing 10 unskilled workers to replace 110 people for the same output volume (Gilbert 1965, p. 6). They were so effective that Gilbert found some of the machines still being used in 1965. Equally, by 1850 almost 6000 miles of railway had been laid and William Huskisson, President of the Board of Trade, expressed the thoughts of many when he argued in 1824 that "if the steam engine be the most powerful instrument in the hands of man to alter the face of the physical world, it operates at the same time as a powerful moral lever in forwarding the great cause of civilisation". Tragically, Huskisson was later killed on 15 September 1830 as Stephenson's Rocket displayed its pace on the Liverpool to Manchester railway.

Although technological advances undoubtedly played a crucial part in the Industrial Revolution, these changes were stimulated by coincidental geo-political events and cultural phenomena. The rapidly growing British empire, enforced by naval power and military occupation, centred around the activities of the East India Company, provided ample sources of low-cost raw materials. It was also a relatively stable period without armed conflict in Europe that allowed for greater levels of British domestic industrial investment. It is also critical to note how many of these innovations were, at least in part, funded from the profits of the Triangular slave trade. For example, slaving ship captain Thomas Hinde used profits from his and his sons' dealings to develop a fabric mill in the village of Dolphinholme in 1795. Even after abolition in 1807, trading with the Americas was crucial to the development of industrial Lancashire: "Every slave in a southern state is an operative for Great Britain . . . and if you will have cotton manufacturers, you must have them based on slave labour" (Thomas Cooper, South Carolina 1830).

Noting the importance of these technological and contextual factors, it was also during this period that advocates of "rational . . . industrial management" (Hobsbawm with Wrigley 1999, p. 101) began to emerge; what we might call proto-OM scholars? Some were industrialists and innovators but also, like the polymath Charles Babbage[7] (Buffa 1980; Landes 1999; Lewis 2003), many were observers and analysts of the sheer breadth of industrial activity taking place during the late 18th – and especially early 19th – century. It is fascinating to note that at this time books describing visits to, and the layouts of, various factories (see for example: Ure 1835; Dodd 1843) "were as popular as earlier works on voyages to distant lands" (Ashworth 1996, p. 631). As Babbage himself argued: "Those who enjoy leisure can scarcely find a more interesting and instructive pursuit than the examination of the workshops of their own country, which contain within them a rich mine of knowledge" (preface to first edition of *On the Economy of Machinery and Manufactures*, January 1832). Critically, Babbage was not content to simply visit, he was someone who "wanted to illuminate his subject by rendering it subject to quantification and calculation" (Rosenberg 1994). Joseph Schumpeter, in his History of Economic Analysis, summarized his skills thus: "he combined a command of simple but sound economic theory with a thorough firsthand knowledge of industrial technology and of the business procedure relevant thereto" (Schumpeter 1955, p. 541). Babbage's book, *On the Economy of Machinery and Manufactures*, was an immediate success, selling out its first edition (so rapidly that Babbage never owned a copy) and was quickly revised and reprinted. Of the original 3000 copies, many have been lost or destroyed – in part through the curious 19th-century habit of saving the title page of a book and discarding the text. Many London booksellers initially boycotted the work because it included an analysis of the expenses in book publishing and distribution (an improper combination of masters against the public). Perhaps the closest contemporary equivalent is the International Motor Vehicle Program (IMVP) report into the performance of the global motor industry: *The Machine That Changed the World* (Womack et al. 1990).

For all this publishing success, it was not until Frederick Winslow Taylor (1856–1915) established his models for the scientific management of business that OM (type) concepts had any consistent impact upon practice (Locke 1982). This was, in part at least, because although England led the process of industrialization (centred on textiles, iron and railways) that took hold in Germany, France, Belgium and the US during the period 1820–1840, by the beginning of the 19th century – American 'labor' productivity was higher than Britain's, despite its lower capital intensity (Broadberry 1994). Within 40 years, the American system of manufacturing (Hounshell 1984) – based in part on the refinement of inter-changeable parts ("the proportion, and relative position, of several parts . . . are so exactly alike; and the screws, springs and other limbs made so similar, that they may be transferred from one . . . and adjusted to another without any material alteration" Dwight 1822) – was perceived to represent global 'best practice' (Wilson 1995, 1996). By 1850, with some US manufacturers (such as Samuel Colt) opening UK production facilities, a UK parliamentary commission investigated the American system and produced a detailed report recommending the adoption of many of its key principles (Rosenberg 1969).

As discussed earlier in relation to the UK industrial revolution, the American system was not simply the summation of various technical components. The US market was 'unhindered' by long-established forms of organizational focus (embodied in structures such as craft guilds and unions) and moved more rapidly towards vertically integrated and larger scale modes of production – a development trajectory that continued until Henry Ford (1863–1947) became the first person to use the system to produce very complex products. State intervention also played an intriguing role with requirements for large quantities of reliable and affordable military equipment leading directly to the sustained work on standardization by private contractors like Eli Whitney and the government armouries at Springfield and Harper's Ferry (Sawyer 1954). Eli Whitney, for instance, accepted his first musket order in 1798 – although at that time he lacked a factory, employees, equipment, finance and any experience of making guns. Whitney was 9 years late delivering on his first federal contract and it was only the exigencies of the 1812 war with Britain that led to a further 15,000 muskets being ordered.

It was Frederick Taylor who eventually distilled these various insights into a series of principles. Over a number of years, he carried out fieldwork looking at jobs (including metal cutting, machine belting, shovelling coal and inspecting ball bearings) and wrote various papers, culminating in his 1911 book, The Principles of Scientific Management. The text advocates a "mental revolution" via the four principles of (1) science over rule of thumb; (2) scientific selection and training; (3) cooperation over individualism; and; (4) an equal division of work best suited to management and employees. It is only really the last of these that seems dated to 21st-century Western sensibilities. Although Scientific Management has been subject to extensive criticism[8] his work undoubtedly influenced management practices in the US, Great Britain, continental Europe, Japan (and the Soviet Union) and continue to have a profound effect on contemporary organization. Critically, Taylor was working at a time when, as US organizations grew in scale and scope, there followed the emergence of an increasingly professional managerial class dedicated to controlling ever more complicated production systems. By the beginning of the 20th century this had created, in North America, a marketplace for formal management education, and operations (scientific) management formed a key part of many curricula (Gordon and Howell 1959). At the same time, engineering education was broadening to include industrial engineering courses, also strongly influenced by Scientific Management principles (Emerson and Naehring 1988). Taylor had a small army of advocates/consultants (i.e., Carl Barth, Henry Gantt, Frank and Lillian Gilbreth), with the Gilbreths in particular playing a key role in the dissemination of the ideas to Japanese industry (Robinson and Robinson 1994).

What then is contemporary OM?

The emergence of what would be readily identifiable as scholarly OM can be traced back to the early 1960s and is often credited to UCLA professor, Ellwood Buffa (Singhal et al. 2007). He was an industrial engineer and, as a UCLA faculty member, part of what in North America by the mid 20th century was a very well-established marketplace for management education, one where Scientific Management formed a key part of many curricula (Gordon and Howell 1959). Whether consciously or not, Buffa was also using terminology that made an explicit link to the adjacent world of Operations (or, in the UK, Operational) Research (OR). The OR field had emerged, and proved itself extremely valuable, during World War II (McCloskey 1987), where its focus had been far wider than the technical challenges of coordinating factory production (aircrew casualty rates, optimal mine locations, etc.). Various rigorous techniques subsequently developed by celebrated people such as George Dantzig (the Simplex Algorithm), Abraham Charnes and William W. Cooper (goal programming and data envelopment analysis, etc.), offered OM a "more scientific" way forward. This was significant because at that time US business school education was being heavily criticized for its lack of rigour.[9] Yet despite this historical proximity (and the border between the fields remains extremely porous, with many OR and OM scholars focused on very similar problems and many OM scholars making extensive use of OR techniques) the relationship is not without its problems. Buffa himself observed that the resultant emphasis on "building a model to represent [practice] and evaluating the results by a single-valued criterion" or, even when building "more complex models [which] we presume are more realistic, since they take into account more variables" could be viewed as having taken OM away from "dealing with the broader managerial implications of decisions in production systems" (Buffa 1980).

Following Buffa's intervention, the newly designated OM field continued to grow in scholarly prominence over the next 20 years or so; albeit some of this growth – in publications, citations, etc. – mirrored a simultaneous decline in 'industrial management' designated work which, given the domination of manufacturing related work, undoubtedly means there was a fair bit of 'old wine in new bottles'. By the 1980s, as the scale and scope of manufacturing changed dramatically (especially in the UK and US economies), Buffa's prescient name change began to have real meaning. The Operations Management Association (OMA), the UK-based scholarly group, was founded at this time (becoming the European OMA in 1993),[10] in part to better reflect the profound shifts that were taking place in economic activity. For example, these esteemed founders[11] believed that OM research needed to better address service operations concerns. That is, those non-manufacturing operations that increasingly represented the vast majority of economic activity (especially in mature economies).

Despite these initiatives, manufacturing and physical good supply chains continued to account for the majority of contemporary OM scholarship. It might be argued that this bias reflects the disproportionately strategic importance that the manufacturing sector has in industrialized and industrializing countries but more plausibly the factory, as a focal point for physical transformation, remains both a peculiarly rich and particularly convenient setting for OM issues and methods.

Of course, in scholarly work, a deliberately narrow frame of reference is not necessarily a bad thing when ecologists want to know how many organisms there are in a particular habitat they drop a quadrat (essentially a small frame) over a smaller plot to isolate a standard unit of area for study of the distribution of an item (plants, insects, etc.) over a larger area. Providing that the sampling and interpretation of results is done with due reflection on broader questions, boundaries, context, etc. such an approach can be invaluable. There is a more worrying corollary of this tight focus, however. Schonberger and Brown (2017) observe, echoing Buffa's earlier comments, that too much effort is expended on questions of localized efficiency to the neglect of broader questions (such as responsiveness in fulfilling customer needs). It should be noted that they also argue that this myopic view of efficiency is reflected in a great deal of contemporary industrial practice!

What about non-manufacturing OM?

Even with manufacturing dominating OM research there is still a significant body of non-manufacturing work to be considered. I will avoid using the S word, in large part because service (ok, so I didn't manage to avoid it!) is such a deeply unhelpful designation. Used in myriad ways, its most straightforward definition is as a noun describing "the action of helping or doing work for someone". Various attempts have been made within (and without) OM to define service but – given that any definition has to cover 70–80% of GDP in most advanced economies, plus nearly all non-market activities – the search for a singular definition seems futile.[12] Of more interest is how attempts at definition can serve to reveal the latent manufacturing orientation and, consequently, relative narrowness of the field. Consider how a manufacturing lens helped shape some key contributions to the service operations literature; Levitt (1972) for example, suggesting that McDonald's had successfully applied a "Production-Line Approach to Service" or Chase (1983) explaining the difference between "front" and "back" office operations. The dominance (until recently) of IHIP[13] (Sasser et al. 1978) is also instructive. These dimensions offer limited insight into the rich and diverse ecology of services, but they do help define some key boundary conditions for manufacturing firms. Despite these conceptual challenges the OM "service imperative" continues to grow (Johnston 1999).

The first part of this imperative we have already highlighted and is pragmatic: manufacturing accounts for a relatively small proportion of GDP in all but a very limited number of (typically emerging) economies. Table 1.1 illustrates the percentage nominal GDP composition (2015 data) of agricultural, industrial and service sectors in a range of countries.

This introduces a quite fundamental disconnect between OM practice and research. Pannirselvam et al. (1999) reviewed 1,754 articles (published 1992–97) in seven key OM journals and identified only 53 (2.7%) articles that addressed service-related themes. This concern has been revisited since (e.g., Roth and Menor 2003), although there has been progress; Smith et al. (2007) analyzed service content in the *Journal of Operations Management* (JOM), *Manufacturing and Service Operations Management* (MSOM), *Production and Operations Management*, *Management Science* (MS) and *Operations Research* (OR) over 17 years (1990–2006) and found that JOM, MSOM and POM all exceeded 15% of service articles during this period. Healthcare, for example, is now a popular 'sector' for OM research (Powell et al. 2012; Dobrzykowski et al. 2014). This is unsurprising, global healthcare systems, from hospitals to social care, face near universal pressures to improve effectiveness and efficiency (Tucker 2007), and consequently 'industrial' methods have – despite an enduring implementation challenge (Nembhard et al. 2009) – significant appeal[14] (McDermott and Stock 2007; Dobrzykowski et al. 2016). Of course, in many ways, healthcare operations (and hospitals in particular) are still very close to manufacturing systems. Likewise, retail systems, with their multi-faceted stock holding problems, generate a significant body of OM work (e.g., Fisher and Raman 2001). Recently, the continued growth of online retailing (and concomitant struggles of real-world retailing!) has prompted lots of research effort into the challenges of so-called omni-channel retailing. All types of retailers now interact with their consumers through multiple channels (Brynjolfsson et al. 2013), but offline and online channels differ markedly in their operational characteristics. Online retail can benefit from lower costs (e.g., via inventory pooling) and forecasting demand for multiple products in multiple store locations is very difficult; with the consequential increase in risk/costs of over/under stocking. Yet at the same time these offline channels have real advantages when it comes to providing information regarding "non-digital attributes" (i.e., the look and feel of a product). The response from online retailers has been to deploy returns process with significant cost implications (including infrastructure/environmental costs). Bell et al. (2015) present an interesting study of

Table 1.1 GDP composition (2015 data)

Country	Nom. GDP ($M)	Agriculture %	Industry %	Service %
United States	17,946,996	1.12	19.1	79.7
United Kingdom	2,649,890	0.7	21	78.3
Germany	3,494,900	0.8	28.1	71.1
China	12,218,281	6.9	40.1	52.9
India	2,250,990	17.4	25.8	56.9

Source: CIA World Factbook.

an emerging hybrid retail mode, whereby an offline showroom allows for efficient information exchange and customer experience whilst maintaining the inventory fulfilment efficiency of online channels. As well as such publications, there are other indications of more service-ness in modern OM.[15] POM now has a service operations college, for instance, and EurOMA has its Service Operations mini-conference, etc., but it remains demonstrably the case that in recent years the most substantive 'turn' in the field has not been to service but rather to supply chains.

Given the detour that we have already taken into the history of manufacturing operations it only seems fair to also recognize pioneering work in service operations as well. Brown and Hyer (2007) present a fantastic overview of what they call archeological benchmarking in their study of the Fred Harvey Company, a highly successful string of restaurants and hotels that began operating in 1876 along the Atchison, Topeka and Santa Fe Railroad. Fred Harvey built an operation that was capable of delivering 15 million meals/year. The firm had a clear operations strategy and built an extraordinary service culture supported by well-trained, loyal employees and underpinned by a sophisticated measurement system (enacted without the advantages of modern information system). Ultimately, Harvey "departed from the traditions of his time to offer mass-customized, high-quality service to the train-traveling middle class" (p. 285).

The second argument for the service OM imperative is actually manufacturing-centric. The growth of an entire sub-field of 'servitization' studies in OM (Baines et al. 2009; Kastalli and Van Looy 2013, etc.) is based on the "recognition that service, how the goods are delivered to the customer and how the customer is treated, provides many manufacturing organizations with a competitive edge". This has echoes of earlier discussions about the 'service factory', where Chase and Garvin (1989) note that "[t]he service tasks of the business can no longer be separated neatly and sequentially from the work of the factory" (p. 69). More broadly, the emergence of various technological platforms only reinforce this blurring of the boundary between physical production assets and the delivery of services.[16]

Given the focus of this text, a third argument relates to the definition of the OM field itself. Just as Buffa was trying to describe the managerial challenges of both manufacturing and non-manufacturing production activities, others have argued that being agnostic with regards to whether you are managing physical and/or non-physical transformations should be axiomatic for OM (Sprague 2007). Although this universality of application is widely asserted, especially in core textbooks, it is perhaps closer to the truth to note that today's scholars are at least dropping the quadrat in a wider range of service locations.

Where's the management?

In his exemplary 2017 overview of OM,[17] Martin Spring asks a profound question, echoing Lee Krajewski's founding JOM editorial: where is the management in operations management? An enduring emphasis on technical analysis, where the key outputs of research are variegated types of optimizing algorithms, a kind of proto-AI if you like, is not worrisome per se, but it becomes more of a cause for concern if elegant solutions become too divorced from their socio-technical setting. There is clearly a tendency, perhaps in the search for analytically and methodologically elegant solutions, to underplay what Martin Starr, again cited by Spring, called the "synthesizing function" (1972, p. vi) of management. There have been periodic concerns regarding the gap between something called practice and something called research (Slack et al. 2004) but the specific, person-centric, concept of management remains under-developed. This is not an exclusive challenge for OM of course; across the business Academy[18] there are worries about the parallel, sometimes even divergent, tracks of scholarship and practice. A former president and editor at the Academy of Management asked: "How long will taxpayers, private and public funding agencies, and society at large tolerate these self-serving, inward-looking 'castle in the sky' research practices?" For OM specifically, consider how Jack Meredith, esteemed scholar, educator and journal editor, recently called for researchers to at least address questions that practitioners could understand! While some suggestions regarding this lack of relevance have been made (Voss 2010), the challenge is arguably ever more acute; as researchers try to balance demands of practice and impact with the needs of increasingly competitive journal publication and promotion/tenure processes.

Crafting a state of the art in OM

The introduction reveals the breadth and depth of the field and this should only serve to confirm that any overview – even if it was possible to agree on a definition of what constitutes the latest/most advanced thinking – will be partial. Given this, I have assembled the content around three personal curating principles. First, to incorporate works that build on, or help to distinguish, fundamental tenets from more transitory fads. Second, to try and better balance non-manufacturing (i.e., given the gravitational pull of the factory, this will not necessarily be a representative sample of the field) and third, to try to keep 'managerial' concerns to the fore. The core content is combined into five thematic areas which are, like this chapter, introduced by analogous discussion of visual art. The text concludes with an attempt at synthesis (*Gesamtkunstwerk?*).

Process

If there is one notion that seems almost universal amidst the myriad components of OM theory and practice, it is the idea of process.[19] Framed as either a noun or a verb, process is the series of actions or steps, bringing together labour, entities and resources to achieve a particular end or specified objective (Hopp et al. 2004). Process is tied to the idea of dependency – typically for OM, flow dependency – whereby capacity, productivity, "wasted" time, etc. is determined through the constraints or bottlenecks in a series of interdependent tasks (of different duration, complexity, etc.). Although powerful and pre-eminent as a perspective, there are limits to this conceptualization, especially when exploring complex service and resource sharing settings. There are actually multiple forms of process dependency, including sharing dependency (when a resource is used for multiple activities), and fit dependency (when multiple activities combine to produce a single resource). There are also ways of thinking about process in a less deterministic way, that engage with the (adjacent) notion of routines and, specifically, open up discussion of generative action (i.e., when systems produce new output, structure or behaviour without input from the originator of the system). Operations fully embraces ideas of emergent behaviour via incremental improvements, *kaizen*, etc., yet the standard simplified conceptualization of process can seem to imply rigidity and mindlessness, and that their content can be explicitly stored somewhere (e.g., a visualization such as a process map). As a result, attempts at (re)designing work are presented as an equally simple matter of creating new, better, rules, procedures and software and that the corresponding material artefacts will determine patterns of action (i.e., software will be used, checklists will get checked and rules will be followed). The gap that then typically emerges between the in-principle design and in-practice action is typically treated as a follow-on phenomenon, rather than intrinsic to the nature of any process.

Planning and control

If process is the unifying construct, then the challenges of planning and control represent the predominant, originating(?), concern of OM over the last century. Since Frank Harris published his seminal 1913 paper asking (and answering!) the question of 'how many parts to make', economic order quantity/volume decisions have been a major research topic. Likewise, there is a direct link between the 1931 introduction of a graphical method to monitor the quality characteristics of process output (by American physicist, engineer and statistician Walter Shewhart) and the application of statistical principles to production control today represented in the 6-sigma movement. In 1935, H F Dodge and H G Romig applied statistical principles to the acceptance and/or rejection of the consignments leading to the field of acceptance sampling. Although queueing theory is typically considered to be part of OR, there are numerous direct connections between the extraordinary insights of Agner Krarup Erlang, the Copenhagen Telephone Exchange engineer who published the first queueing theory paper in 1909. His modelling of the number of telephone calls arriving at an exchange by a Poisson process has had significant impact in a range of prototypical OM applications including industrial engineering and the design of call centres, hospitals, server farms, etc. In short, analytical and heuristic optimization of multiple production planning variables was, and remains, a major focus of OM research activity.

People

OM has long recognized the impact of human behaviour on operating systems. FW Taylor studied the simple output to time relationship for manual labour such as brick-laying. This formed the precursor of the present-day 'time study'. Around the same time, Frank and Lillian Gilbreth examined the motions of the limbs of the workers (such as the hands, legs, eyes, etc.) in performing the jobs and tried to standardize these motions into certain categories and utilize the classification to arrive at standards for time required to perform a given job. This was the precursor to the present-day 'motion study'. It was arguably not until the series of experiments that took place at Western Electric's factory at Hawthorne, a suburb of Chicago, in the late 1920s and early 1930s, that scholars began to think differently about work and productivity. Taylor's influential ideas were focused on the individual, whereas the work of Elton Mayo, an Australian-born sociologist who eventually became a professor of industrial research at Harvard, emphasized the individual in their social context, establishing that employees are influenced by their surroundings and by the people that they are working with. The experimenters ultimately concluded that it was not the changes in physical conditions that were affecting the workers' productivity (i.e., how bright the lights were), rather it was the fact that someone was actually concerned about the conditions in the workplace, and the opportunities this gave them to discuss changes before they took place.

In these early works, the worker is treated more or less like a sophisticated machine. It is only relatively recently that (in some areas) OM has started to become an overtly behavioural discipline; one that reflects more fully on the way that people make (and avoid) decisions and interact (and fight) with each other. Of course, recent attempts to better align OM research with more "realistic" assumptions about human cognition, emotion and social interaction via wholesale importation of concepts and ideas from adjacent disciplines is not without risk – in particular given that psychology is itself undergoing a significant period of self-criticism and reflection.

Strategy and measures

Operations strategy (OS) is a potentially paradoxical idea. If a firm has an OS, this typically that forms part of a cluster of strategy elements (marketing, finance, HR strategy, etc.) which, in theory, should combine to achieve the wider goals and strategies of the business. The overall model of strategy invoked is significant. Adopting a 'top-down' model of strategy implies OS is primarily about alignment and implementation (cf. Skinner 1974), whereas most contemporary scholars draw heavily on Henry Mintzberg's notion of strategy as more than just intended or planned strategy but also emergent "pattern of actions" and "sequence of decisions". Questions regarding measures and measurement are also profoundly intertwined with considerations of OS. Measures are used as a proxy for operations performance (cost, quality, speed, etc.) but also frequently as a substitute for a richer engagement with the OS process.

Technology

Any perspective on OM needs to incorporate the (paradoxical) role played by technology. Technology allows firms to scale, to control, to achieve extraordinary efficiencies but also helps to de-skill work, reduce wage rates, reduce training requirements, etc. Moreover, researching the use, effects and impacts of a relatively new – and constantly changing – set of technologies is different to the questions of adoption and adaptation that predominate in a more mature and stable technology landscape. Consider how much of what was interesting to research at the turn of the Millennium (e.g., Enterprise Resource Planning, ERP, systems based on 'traditional' centralized, database type technologies) and was consequently the focus of much research in both the OM and IS communities (e.g., Kumar and Hillegersberg 2000; Nah and Zuckweiler 2003; Cotteleer and Bendoly 2006) is increasingly irrelevant today. OM research needs to be cognizant of the prevalence and state of development of technology because rapid technological change is not only throwing up significant new and different research opportunities, it is fundamentally challenging the core assumptions of the field.

Synthesis and suggestions for a future state of the art?

In the last chapter of the book, an attempt is made to draw together these different strands, again not to identify a singular 'state of the art' but rather to draw creative inspiration from the various, often contradictory, perspectives presented. Here again the history of art proves instructive; it is replete with various attempts at uniting very different art forms into an artistic whole.[20] For example, architecture and art are often united, as are poetry and music or the introduction of feature films into an art gallery, etc. OM is in many ways a 'mash up' discipline anyway and in this final section there is extended reflection on the implications of borrowing so heavily from adjacent fields. This leads on to discussion of, the inevitable yin and yang of management research, how to balance connections to practice (with specific reference to the challenge of environmental sustainability) with the need for ever greater analytical rigour? The chapter does attempt some constructive synthesis of its own, exploring a topic that is implicit across all the text but perhaps insufficiently considered as an OM topic in its own right – the role of time and temporality. To finish, there is a brief discussion of how OM might answer the contemporary challenges of open science.

Notes

1 "State of the art" dates to 1910 and an engineering text by Henry Harrison Suplee. He used the term to refer to the 'useful' arts, skills and methods relating to subjects such as manufacturing.
2 Although it is worth noting that OM practice and scholarship is replete with discussion of the role of the visual and the process of visualization: control and Gantt charts, process maps, kanban squares, obeya rooms, andon status lights, etc.
3 One of the most celebrated curators, Hans Ulrich Obrist, director of the Serpentine Galleries in London, argues that, in addition to displaying or arranging works and identifying new work, curating also involves safeguarding heritage and connecting to art history.

4 The original version of the picture of the Arsenale was purchased in 1736 by the 4th Duke of Bedford and today hangs in the Dining Room at Woburn Abbey, UK.

5 The word, manufacture, has developed from meaning 'make by hand' to 'make by machine or by industrial process'.

6 Galileo Galilei was, from 1593, a consultant at the Arsenale, responsible for numerous technological and logistical innovations.

7 Babbage today is best known for his machines designed to calculate mathematical tables. In 1824, he received the first gold medal awarded by the Astronomical Society for his work on these difference engines. In 1834 he began work on an ultimately fruitless attempt to construct an automatic general-purpose analytical engine, retrospectively claimed as the forerunner of the modern digital computer.

8 In 1914 a US House of Representatives committee investigated his plant management system. Although the committee found no evidence of abuse and no legislation was passed (a bill was proposed), scientific management inevitably lost some credibility along the way.

9 The Ford Foundation "Higher Education for Business" report by Gordon and Howell was one of two reports on business education published in 1959 (the other being Frank Pierson's Carnegie Foundation funded "The Education of American Businessmen: A Study of University-College Programmes in Business Administration"). Gordon and Howell offered a fundamental critique of the business school world: academics as quacks; poor students; narrow, simple and weak curricula. The report called for more research and less faculty consulting work, better regulation, fewer case studies, more theory and analysis and more teaching of ethics.

10 Kalyan Singhal founded the North American Production & Operations Management Society on June 30, 1989.

11 For those interested in such trivia, the OMA was formed in 1984 following a meeting (between Nigel Slack, Chris Voss, Bob Johnston and Colin Armistead) at The Volunteer public house, near London Business School.

12 That is not to say there are no useful definitional models. Lovelock (1983) classified services against multiple dimensions. The nature of the service act? The type of relationship with customers? How much room is there for service provider customization and judgement? What is the nature of demand and supply? How is the service delivered? Similarly, and from within OM, work by Hopp and Liu (2009) more precisely defines the nature of labour input to a process by defining the difference between blue and white collar work (Intellectual vs. Physical and Creative vs. Routine).

13 Intangibility, Heterogeneity, Inseparability (simultaneity of production and consumption) and Perishability.

14 These systems are also data rich and amendable to the increasingly sophisticated analytical techniques that characterize 'state of the art' OM scholarship.

15 For example, Aksin et al. (2007) OM in the then 'modern' call centre, while Karwan and Markland (2006) investigated public services (in their case the US Department of Motor Vehicles). Similarly, Hopp and Liu (2009) and Harvey et al. (2016) have highlighted some of the unique challenges associated with Professional Services OM.

16 Intriguingly, ground-breaking economist Edith Penrose, in her *Theory of the Growth of the Firm*, touched upon this relationship when she argued that "[a] resource . . . can be viewed as a bundle of possible services" (Penrose 1959, p. 67).

17 Chapter 4 in Wilkinson, A., Armstrong, S. J., & Lounsbury, M. (Eds.). (2017). *The Oxford Handbook of Management*. Oxford: Oxford University Press.

18 Various articles such as "Connecting Scholars and Business" (BizEd Editorial Staff 2014).

19 Most framing definitions propose that OM is concerned with the processes involved in delivering goods and services to customers (Spearman and Hopp 1996).

20 As so often there is a German word, Gesamtkunstwerk, that can be translated as "total work of art" or "synthesis of the arts". It is a work of art that makes use of all or many art forms.

Bibliography

Aksin, Z., Armony, M., & Mehrotra, V. (2007). The modern call center. *Production and Operations Management*, 16(6), 665–688.

Ashworth, W. J. (1996). Memory, efficiency, and symbolic analysis: Charles Babbage, John Herschel, and the industrial mind. *Isis*, 87(4), 629–653.

Baines, T. S., Lightfoot, H. W., Benedettini, O., & Kay, J. M. (2009). The servitization of manufacturing: A review of literature and reflection on future challenges. *Journal of Manufacturing Technology Management*, 20(5), 547–567.

Bell, D., Gallino, S., & Moreno, A. (2015). Showrooms and information provision in omnichannel retail. *Production and Operations Management*, 24(3), 360–362.

Berg, M. (1994). *The Age of Manufactures, 1700–1820: Industry, Innovation, and Work*. Routledge, New York.

Boone, T., & Ganeshan, R. (2001). The effect of information technology on learning in professional service organizations. *Journal of Operations Management*, 19(4), 485–495.

Boyer, K. K., Gardner, J. W., & Schweikhart, S. (2012). Process quality improvement: An examination of general vs. outcome-specific climate and practices in hospitals. *Journal of Operations Management*, 30(4), 325–339.

Broadberry, S. N. (1994). Comparative productivity in British and American manufacturing during the nineteenth century. In: *Explorations in Economic History*, vol. 31, no. 3, Academic Press, pp. 521–548.

Broekhuis, M., & Pieter van Donk, D. (2011). Coordination of physicians' operational activities: A contingency perspective. *International Journal of Operations & Production Management*, 31(3), 251–273.

Brown, K. A., & Hyer, N. L. (2007). Archeological benchmarking: Fred Harvey and the service profit chain, Circa 1876. *Journal of Operations Management*, 25(2), 284–299.

Brynjolfsson, E., Hu, Y. J., & Rahman, M. (2013). Competing in the age of omnichannel retailing. *Sloan Management Review*, 54(4), 21–29.

Buffa, E. S. (1980). Research in operations management. *Journal of Operations Management*, 1(1), 1–7.

Carmona, S., Ezzamel, M., & Gutiérrez, F. (1997). Control and cost accounting practices in the Spanish Royal Tobacco Factory. *Accounting, Organizations and Society*, 22(5), 411–446.

Chase, R. B., Garvin, D. A. (1989). The service factory. *Harvard Business Review*, 67(4), 61–69.

Chase, R. B., & Tansik, D. A. (1983). The customer contact model for organization design. *Management Science*, 29(9), 1037–1050.

Cook, L. S., Bowen, D. E., Chase, R. B., Dasu, S., Stewart, D. M., & Tansik, D. A. (2002). Human issues in service design. *Journal of Operations Management*, 20(2), 159–174.

Cooper, C. C. (1981). The production line at Portsmouth block mill. *Industrial Archaeology Review*, 6(1), 28–44.

Cotteleer, M. J., & Bendoly, E. (2006). Order lead-time improvement following enterprise information technology implementation: an empirical study. *MIS Quarterly*, 643–660.

Dobrzykowski, D. D., Deilami, V. S., Hong, P., & Kim, S. C. (2014). A structured analysis of operations and supply chain management research in healthcare (1982–2011). *International Journal of Production Economics*, 147, 514–530.

Dobrzykowski, D. D., McFadden, K. L., & Vonderembse, M. A. (2016). Examining pathways to safety and financial performance in hospitals: A study of lean in professional service operations. *Journal of Operations Management*, 42, 39–51.

Dodd, G. (1843). *Days at the Factories: Or, The Manufacturing Industry of Great Britain Described, and Illustrated by Numerous Engravings of Machines and Processes. Series I.-London.* C. Knight & Company.

Dwight, T. (1822). *Travels in New England and New York*, vol. 4. New Haven.

Emerson, H. P., Naehring, D. C. E. (1988). *The Origins of Industrial Engineering*. Institute of Industrial Engineers, Norcross, GA.

Fisher, M., & Raman, A. (2001). Introduction to focused issue: Retail operations management. *Manufacturing & Service Operations Management*, 3(3), 189–190.

Gilbert, K. R. (1965). *The Portsmouth block-making machinery: a pioneering enterprise in mass production*. HM Stationery Office.

Gordon, R. A., Howell, J. E. (1959). *Higher Education for Business*. Columbia University Press, NY.

Harris, F. W. (1913). How many parts to make at once. *The Magazine of Management*, 10(2), 135–136.

Harvey, J., Heineke, J., & Lewis, M. (2016). Editorial for journal of operations management special issue on Professional Service Operations Management (PSOM). *Journal of Operations Management*.

Hobsbawm, E. J., & Wrigley, C. (1999). *Industry and Empire: from 1750 to the Present Day*. The New Press.

Hopp, I., & Liu. (2009). Managing white-collar work. *Production and Operations Management*, 18(1), 1–32.

Hopp, W. J., Tekin, E., & Van Oyen, M. P. (2004). Benefits of skill chaining in serial production lines with cross-trained workers. *Management Science*, 50(1), 83–98.

Hounshell, D. (1984). *From the American System to Mass Production, 1800–1934*. John Hopkins University Press, Baltimore, MD.

Johnston, R. (1999). Service operations management: return to roots. International *Journal of Operations & Production Management*, 19(2), 104–124.

Karwan, K. R., & Markland, R. E. (2006). Integrating service design principles and information technology to improve delivery and productivity in public sector operations: The case of the South Carolina DMV. *Journal of Operations Management*, 24(4), 347–362.

Kastalli, I. V., & Van Looy, B. (2013). Servitization: Disentangling the impact of service business model innovation on manufacturing firm performance. *Journal of Operations Management*, 31(4), 169–180.

Ketokivi, M., & McIntosh, C. N. (2017). Addressing the endogeneity dilemma in operations management research: Theoretical, empirical, and pragmatic considerations. *Journal of Operations Management*.

Kleindorfer, P. R., Singhal, K., & Wassenhove, L. N. (2005). Sustainable operations management. *Production and Operations Management*, 14(4), 482–492.

Kumar, K., & Van Hillegersberg, J. (2000). ERP experiences and evolution. *Communications of the ACM*, 43(4), 22–22.

Landes, D. (1999). *The Wealth and Poverty of Nations: Why Some Are So Rich and Some So Poor*. Norton, New York.

Lane, F. C. (1934) Venetian Naval Architecture about 1550, *The Mariner's Mirror*, 20(1), 24–49.

Lane, F., & Lane, F. C. (1973). *Venice, a maritime republic*. JHU Press.

Levitt, T. (1972). Production-line approach to service. *Harvard business review, 50*(5), 41–52.

Lewis, M. A. (2007). Charles Babbage: Reclaiming an operations management pioneer. *Journal of Operations Management*, 25(2), 248–259.

Locke, E. (1982). The ideas of Frederick Taylor: an evaluation. Academy of Management Review 7, 14–24.

Lovelock, C. H. (1983). Classifying services to gain strategic marketing insights. *Journal of marketing, 47*(3), 9–20.

Martinón-Torres, M., et al. (2014). Forty thousand arms for a single emperor: From chemical data to the labor organization behind the bronze arrows of the terracotta army. *Journal of Archaeological Method and Theory*, 21(3), 534–562.

McCloskey, J. F. (1987). OR forum: The beginnings of operations research: 1934–1941. *Operations Research*, 35(1), 143–152.

McDermott, C., & Stock, G. N. (2007). Hospital operations and length of stay performance. *International Journal of Operations & Production Management*, 27(9), 1020–1042.

McIvor, R. (2009). How the transaction cost and resource-based theories of the firm inform outsourcing evaluation. *Journal of Operations Management*, 27(1), 45–63.

Nah, F. F. H., Zuckweiler, K. M., & Lee-Shang Lau, J. (2003). ERP implementation: chief information officers' perceptions of critical success factors. *International journal of Human-computer Interaction*, 16(1), 5–22.

Nembhard, I. M., Alexander, J. A., Hoff, T. J., & Ramanujam, R. (2009). Why does the quality of health care continue to lag? Insights from management research. *The Academy of Management Perspectives*, 23(1), 24–42.

Pannirselvam, G. P., Ferguson, L. A., Ash, R. C., & Siferd, S. P. (1999). Operations management research: an update for the 1990s. *Journal of Operations Management*, 18(1), 95–112.

Penrose, E. (1959)."The theory of the growth of the firm." John Wiley & Sons, New York.

Powell, A., Savin, S., & Savva, N. (2012). Physician workload and hospital reimbursement: Overworked physicians generate less revenue per patient. *Manufacturing & Service Operations Management*, 14(4), 512–528.

Robinson, A. G., Robinson, M. M. (1994). On the tabletop improvement experiments of Japan. *Production and Operations Management*, 3(3), 201–216.

Rosenberg, N. (Ed.) (1969). *The American System of Manufactures*. Edinburgh University Press, Edinburgh.

Rosenberg, N. (1994). Babbage: pioneer economist. In: Rosenberg, N. (Ed.), *Exploring the Black Box: Technology, Economics and History*. Cambridge University Press, Cambridge, UK (Chapter 2).

Roth, A. V., & Menor, L. J. (2003). Insights into service operations management: A research agenda. *Production and Operations Management*, 12(2), 145–164.

Sampson, S. E., & Froehle, C. M. (2006). Foundations and implications of a proposed unified services theory. *Production and Operations Management*, 15(2), 329–343.

Sasser, W. E., Olsen, R. P., & Wyckoff, D. D. (1978). *Management of Service Operations: Text, Cases, and Readings*. Allyn & Bacon.

Sawyer, J. E. (1954). The social basis of the American system of manufacturing. *Journal of Economic History*, 14(4), 361–379.

Schonberger, R. J., & Brown, K. A. (2017). Missing link in competitive manufacturing research and practice: customer-responsive concurrent production. *Journal of Operations Management*, 49, 83–87.

Schumpeter, J. A. (1955). *A History of Economic Analysis*. Oxford University Press.

Simpson, D., Meredith, J., Boyer, K., Dilts, D., Ellram, L. M., & Leong, G. K. (2015). Professional, research, and publishing trends in operations and supply chain management. *Journal of Supply Chain Management*, 51(3), 87–100.

Singhal, K., Singhal, J., & Starr, M. K. (2007). The domain of production and operations management and the role of Elwood Buffa in its delineation. *Journal of Operations Management*, 25(2), 310–327.

Skinner, W. (1974). The focused factory. *Harvard Business Review*, 114–121.

Slack, N., Lewis, M., & Bates, H. (2004). The two worlds of operations management research and practice: can they meet, should they meet?. *International Journal of Operations & Production Management*, 24(4), 372–387.

Smith, J. S., Karwan, K. R., & Markland, R. E. (2007). A note on the growth of research in service operations management. *Production and Operations Management*, 16(6), 780–790.

Spearman, M. L., & Hopp, W. J. (1996). *Factory Physics: Foundations of Manufacturing Management*. Irwin, Chicago, IL.

Sprague, L. G. (2007). Evolution of the field of operations management. *Journal of Operations Management*, 25(2), 219–238.

Starr, M. K. (1972). *Production management; systems and synthesis*. Prentice Hall.

Starr, M. K., & Van Wassenhove, L. N. (2014). Introduction to the special issue on humanitarian operations and crisis management. *Production and Operations Management*, 23(6), 925–937.

Tucker, A. L. (2007). An empirical study of system improvement by frontline employees in hospital units. *Manufacturing & Service Operations Management*, 9(4), 492–505.

Ulrich, K. (1995). The role of product architecture in the manufacturing firm. *Research Policy*, 24(3), 419–440.

Ure, A. (1835). *The Philosophy of Manufactures: Or, An Exposition of the Scientific, Moral and Commercial Economy of the Factory System of Great Britain*, Charles Knight, London.

van Aken, J., Chandrasekaran, A., & Halman, J. (2016). Conducting and publishing design science research: Inaugural essay of the design science department of the journal of operations management. *Journal of Operations Management*, 47, 1–8.

Voss, C. A. (2007). Learning from the first operations management textbook. *Journal of Operations Management*, 25(2), 239–247.

Voss, C. A. (2010). Reflections on the state of OM. *POM Chronicle*, 17(1), 11–12.

Wilson, J. M. (1995). An historical perspective on operations management. *Production and Inventory Management Journal*, 61–66 (Third Quarter).

Wilson, J. M. (1996). A comparison of the 'American system of manufactures' circa 1850 with just in time methods. *Journal of Operations Management*, 16, 77–90.

Womack, J., Jones, D. T., Roos, D. (1990). *The Machine That Changed the World*. Rawson Associates, New York, NY.

Zan, L. (2004). Accounting and management discourse in proto-industrial settings: the Venice Arsenal in the turn of the 16th century. *Accounting and Business Research*, 34(2), 145–175.

2   Process

A huge canvas by celebrated abstract expressionist Jackson Pollock confronts you as you enter the first of our imaginary galleries. Measuring 2.4 × 1.2 m (8 × 4 ft), No. 5 is a "dense bird's nest" of a painting that was created by dripping and flicking grey, brown, white and yellow liquid gloss enamel paints onto fibreboard.[1] Although poorly received when it was created, the artwork sold in May 2006 for $140 million, at that time the most ever paid for any painting.[2] No. 5 is a key example of 'process' art, whereby influential post-war artists engaged with concepts of time, timing, change and transience, making the key subject of many pieces the crafting of the work itself. Just as Jackson Pollock dripped and poured successive layers of paint onto canvas, his actions in making the work could be clearly understood and, to some extent, reconstructed.[3]

This idea of process – deployed as either a noun or a verb – describing the sequence of actions/events that bring together people, information and other resources in the pursuit of specified objectives (Hopp et al. 2004) is arguably as close as OM comes to a unifying concept. The field relies on activity/event sequences as a mechanism for description (i.e., mapping what is going on, etc.), to establish practical and theoretical connections between cause and effect (i.e., the why and how)[4] and propose interventions to modify systemic behaviour(s). Beyond its descriptive value, process 'management', specifically the challenge of variability reduction, represents a key part of the OM canon (especially under the rubric of quality management). This typically involves "concerted efforts to map, improve, and adhere to organizational processes" (Benner and Tushman 2003), where 'improvement and adherence' means the deliberate reduction of process variety (e.g., reducing the standard deviation of some key variable) to better control outcomes. It is also one of the topics where OM concerns broke through into the wider business ecosystem. Ever since advocates of business process re-engineering, BPR, called for companies to 'obliterate' their processes (Hammer and Champy 1993), the impact of such ideas on the business community and OM research has been profound. Although well past its faddish peak in scholarly terms, BPR is 'alive and well' in practice; a core element of international quality-related initiatives, including the International Organization for Standardization's Series 9000 programme (ISO 9000), the Malcolm Baldrige National Quality Award, and, more recently, Six Sigma programmes.

Specialization

As discussed in the introduction, the division of labour, task specialization, co-ordination, etc. have played a central role in the evolution of human society. In the first chapter of *An Inquiry into the Nature and Causes of the Wealth of Nations* (1776, p. 7) for instance, Adam Smith articulated three specific advantages that accrue to the firm from the division of labour: increased "dexterity in every particular work-man", saving time lost in "passing from one species of work to another", and the application of labour-saving technologies that enable "one man to do the work of many". Charles Babbage helped to clarify the exact nature of this advantage:[5]

> [T]he master manufacturer by dividing the work to be executed into different processes, each requiring different degrees of skill or of force can purchase exactly that precise quantity of both which is necessary for each process; whereas, if the whole work were to be executed by one workman, that person must possess sufficient skill to perform the most difficult, and sufficient strength to execute the most laborious, of the operations into which the art is divided.
>
> (On the Economy of Machinery and Manufactures, 1832, pp. 175–6)

> But if a manufacturer insist on employing one man to make the whole needle, he must pay at the rate of five pounds a week for every portion of the labour bestowed upon it.
>
> (Babbage 1864, p. 328)

Frederick Taylor further distilled this insight with his principles of Scientific Management which included (but were not limited to, see Locke 1982 for a thorough review) breaking down a task, optimizing individual stages and then focusing worker (selection, tools, incentives) to find the 'one best way' to repeatedly complete the task (Taylor 1911).

Since that time, scholars have continued to debate whether productivity is higher when work is specialized or varied. Specialization can assist workers gain (faster, deeper) skills in a particular task and limit the distracting effects of task changeovers (Schultz et al. 2003), a question that has become ubiquitous in recent years with the distractions that arise from being constantly connected to multiple streams of content via digital work tools (Rosen and Samuel 2015). More specifically, there is strong evidence that if a worker is required to undertake many short-cycle tasks, where variety can be distracting, specialization helps. There are also potential 'dis-benefits' associated with specialization. Researchers (e.g., Walker and Guest 1952) began to show that these narrow, 'scientific' jobs led many employees to behave in ways – including lateness and lack of attention to detail – that actually undermined any theoretical efficiency gains (see Oldham and Fried 2016 for a comprehensive review of the last 50 years of job design research). Engaging in a variety of tasks can improve motivation (Fried and Ferris 1987), especially when a worker has repeatedly completed a task (Ortega 2001), and engagement and 'adjacent' task knowledge can be invaluable (Tucker et al. 2007). Although we should note that much of this research remains anchored in the factory (or service factory) and the types of self-paced, self-actualizing knowledge work that increasingly characterize modern organizations are under-researched (cf. KC and Terwiesch 2009), it is likely that some balance between the two strategies (the goldilocks zone of task variety/specialization?) will prove effective in many settings.

Practitioners have also engaged with this challenge, perhaps most (in)famously, in the Uddevalla, Sweden assembly plant opened by Volvo in 1989. At the time the plant manager boasted: "This isn't just new production technology. It is the death of the assembly line" (*Business Week*, August 28, 1989). The plant deployed multiple small parallel teams to build complete cars with individual task cycle times ranging from 1.5 to 7 hours (cf. the approx. 2 minutes that are typical on a contemporary vehicle assembly line). The plant achieved significant scholarly celebrity and was visited many times with many embracing its idiosyncrasies but others (*New York Times*, July 7 1991) concluding that the plant was doomed to failure, since "assembly lines are just more efficient". In the same article James Womack, at the MIT, asserted that Uddevalla was "a dead horse". Uddevalla would eventually be shut down in 1993 – its actual performance and legacy remain disputed (e.g., Berggren 1994; Adler and Cole 1994).

Bottlenecks and flow

In a given sequence of events, the performance or capacity of the 'system' can be limited by a single or small number of components or resources (i.e., those that are relatively slow or unreliable, or unavailable, etc.). Consequently, a great deal of OM activity has focused on improving – by eliminating or by better managing – dependencies. If a bottleneck cannot be eliminated in some way, say by adding capacity, productivity can be augmented by maintaining consistent production through it, if need be with long runs and few changeovers. Non-bottleneck operations do not require long runs and few changeovers. Throughput time, a measure of the speed of the flow from the point where "materials for a unit of the product are first worked on until that unit is completed and supplied to either the customer or to a finished goods warehouse" (Schmenner and Swink 1998, p. 102), is typically used to capture the impact of the bottleneck on an operation. The term bottleneck, which literally refers to that narrow top part of a bottle that determines the rate of pour, is used figuratively in many settings. From a local disruption in a transport network, to Liebig's law of the minimum where, in agricultural science (and modelling populations and ecological systems, etc.), growth is not limited by the total resources available, but rather by the scarcest resource.[6] Similarly, Thomas P. Hughes, the eminent American historian of technology, used a version of the bottleneck concept (he uses the term reverse salients[7]) in his analysis of how technological systems are prevented from achieving targeted performance as the result of insufficient development in a specific component of the system.

Today, the bottleneck is probably most readily associated with the works of Goldratt (Goldratt and Cox 1984, Goldratt 1989) and his 'theory of constraints'

(TOC); every process has a single constraint, total process throughput can only be improved when the constraint is improved and, consequently, spending time optimizing non-constraints will not provide significant benefits. Only improvements to the constraint will further, what Goldratt described as, The Goal (i.e., achieving more profit). Much of the evolution of this bottleneck-centric philosophy, subsequently focused on the individual and organizational response to its principles. For example, as Watson et al. (2007) describe in their comprehensive review of the evolution of TOC, workers would sometimes ignore OPT-generated schedules because

> they kept some stations efficiently busy while others were idle at times. The whole approach contradicted the performance measurement systems in place at most US plants, as workers were usually measured by individual efficiency . . . [and therefore they would] produce parts for inventory in an attempt to stay busy and avoid unfavorable performance appraisals. These actions created unsynchronized material flows through the plant, scrambling the schedule and endangering the success of OPT itself.
>
> (p. 390)

In other words, arguably the key challenge of seeking maximum utilization of a bottleneck constraint is in reducing the activation of non-constraint resources. TOC highlights three forms of constraint: physical (resource capacity less than demand), market (demand less than resource capacity), and policy (formal or informal rules that limit productive capacity of the system). This is a theme that also features as a central aspect of the Toyota Production System.

Goldratt's subsequent focus on managerial education led to the publication, together with Jeff Cox, of *The Goal*, the first of a series of novels (*It's Not Luck* (1994), *The Critical Chain* (1997), *Necessary but Not Sufficient* (2000), etc.) designed to convey managerial lessons. *The Goal* became one of the best-selling business books ever written (on the cover of its 2014, 30th anniversary edition, North River Press claimed the book had sold more than 6 million copies). The book tells the story of how plant manager Alex Rogo is helped along the path to a higher level of bottleneck consciousness by the Socratic methods of his mentor, Jonah. The book also first outlined the drum-buffer-rope (DBR) scheduling methodology.[8] Both the general philosophy and specific technical aspects of TOC approach (such as DBR) has been – and continues to be – extensively covered in the literature (e.g., Rahman 1998; Golmohammadi 2015; Thurer et al. 2017) including a broad literature comparing DBR with Material Requirements Planning (MRP), infinite loading, and kanban/JIT systems (e.g., Gupta and Snyder 2009). Although the term 'buffer' has become, post Lean, increasingly pejorative, synonymous with the negative aspects of work-in-process or finished goods inventory, TOC advocates actively managing dependencies by deploying three distinct buffer types: time (an offset protection for critical resources), shipping (to protect due date performance), and capacity (at non-bottlenecks).

An important corollary of bottleneck management is the desire to achieve flow. Widely used to describe mathematical and physical phenomenon, its application to the world of work (workflow) remains aligned with the notion of something (e.g., a liquid, gas, electricity, or a manufactured artefact, piece of information, customer, etc.) moving steadily and continuously in a current or stream. Insights developed from queuing theory, with its rich multi-disciplinary heritage (OR/MS, mathematics, engineering, etc.), have major implications for considerations of flow. For instance, in describing a single server queue system, three elements (process time, arrival and service variability, and utilisation) are typically combined to define queue time. In their reflections on the nature of theory in OM, Schmenner and Swink (1998) observe that the "more variable the timing or the nature of the jobs to be done by the process, and the more variable the processing steps themselves or the items processed, and correspondingly, the less output there will be from the process". They develop this observation to propose what they call the Theory of Swift, Even Flow (SEF). This adds dimensionality to the general concepts of "continuously and steadily" by positing that the more 'swift and even' the flow through a process, the more productive that process is. It is also interesting to note at this point, that the idea of flow has also found a home in the world of (work – and sport, artistic, etc.) psychology, where it was first defined by psychologist Mihaly Csikszentmihályi[9] as a situation where individuals act with a sense of total control, concentration, deep involvement and enjoyment. In order to achieve such a state of flow, Csikszentmihályi laid out three conditions (goals are clear; feedback is immediate; and, there is a balance between opportunity and capacity) that are evidently analogous to OMs insights regarding task variety and specialization discussed earlier. To explain SEF theory, Schmenner and Swink (1998) argue that it is necessary to understand a series of associated theoretical concepts. The first of these, how bottlenecks are an impediment to flow, we have discussed earlier. The second is how variability – associated with either the demand on the process (Ca) or with the process's operations steps (Cs) can drive the creation of queues and backlogs (especially in settings where there are high levels of capacity utilization) and become an impediment to flow. To increase flow therefore, variability should be narrowed and consequently, stable and level production plans (with lower variance in both timing and quantities demanded) are more compatible with higher levels of productivity. If all work processes were fixed (tasks, sequence, resources, etc.[10]), then the problem of process variability would be largely addressed by the array of long-established tools and statistical techniques for doing just that.

Too much flow?

There has been interesting work suggesting an over emphasis on flow dependency in OM, especially in collaborative, multitasking workflows that involve indivisible resources (prototypically 'white collar' work: Hopp and Liu 2009). In short, although "[m]ost operations management textbooks use the following simple approximation to illustrate the computation of the capacity of a process: the capacity of each resource is first calculated by examining that resource in isolation; process capacity is then defined as the smallest among the capacities of the resources, that is, bottleneck capacity" (Bo et al. 2018), there are actually multiple forms of potentially opposed process dependency, including resource sharing and fit dependencies (Malone and Crowston 1994). In collaborative 'networks', where many tasks are processed by indivisible (human or otherwise) multitasking resources (e.g., a treatment pathway requiring a combination of healthcare professionals), the traditional "bottleneck formula" can be inaccurate (Gurvich and Van Mieghem 2015). The capacity of such networks is often smaller than the bottleneck capacity depending on the level of collaboration required by the task. Gurvich and Van Mieghem (2018) further conclude that to maximize the capacity of a collaborative network, highest priority must be given to the tasks that require the most collaboration, an attractive decentralized policy but one which they themselves note "has consequences for organizational and network design".

Waste

Schmenner and Swink highlight a third flow variable: the balance of value-added and non-value-added work. Work that "transforms materials into good product is considered value-added, while work that moves materials, catalogues them, inspects them, counts them, or reworks them is not regarded as value-added" (p. 102). Following this logic, a process becomes more 'swift and even' when non-value-added steps of the process are either eliminated or greatly reduced. This notion of non-value adding work, and its conceptual twin, the notion of waste, has its roots in the Toyota Production System (TPS). Taiichi Ohno called TPS a management system for "the absolute elimination of waste" and industrial consultant (and famous popularizer of TPS), Shigeo Shingo,[11] famously proposed a typology of (seven) production wastes – overproduction, waiting, transportation, unnecessary processing, stocks, motions and defects. These wastes have subsequently become a central tenet of contemporary OM. More recently, Poppendieck and Poppendieck (2006) 'translated' these seven wastes to software development processes (Partially Done Work, Extra Features, Relearning, Handoffs, Delays, Task Switching, and Defects) and other additional forms of waste have been suggested. Womack and Jones (1996) have noted, for example, that "the design of goods and services that don't meet the users' needs" is a form of waste and/or that the underutilization of employee skills or complexity is the eighth waste.

Service processes

Talk of queueing and the production of software leads us to consideration of those processes that include the customer as an integral part of the transformation (Chase 1978; Sampson & Froehle 2006). The terminology can be slightly different. Collier and Meyer (1998, p. 1232) for example, talk about the "service encounter activity sequence", meaning all the steps and associated encounters necessary to complete a service transaction and fulfil a customer's wants and needs. Consider a visit to an art gallery. It clearly consists of a sequence of activities and experiences: paying for a ticket, buying an audio guide, viewing, walking, sitting, waiting, choosing gifts in the shop, etc. In evaluating this as a process we might ask, how long does each stage take? Where are the queues? How much resource is needed at each stage? Alternatively, many OM scholars add significant depth by adopting a psychologically informed perspective (Cook et al. 2002; Chase and Dasu 2001). Consider how satisfaction derived from a pleasant experience may actually be higher when the experience is interrupted by an annoying break than with no interruption (Nelson & Meyvis 2008) or how a long queue that ends with a very rapid advance may result in a more positive retrospective evaluation than just having experienced a shorter queue (Carmon et al. 1995). From a customer/service process perspective not all stages are equally important. People tend to forget past events more than recent ones and this 'memory decay' has an impact. When queuing, customers become gradually demoralized as they wait, but then positively respond to each advance of the queue (Carmon et al. 1995). Marketing and psychological research suggest that customers summarize their experiences based on three key characteristics. Sequence matters (Dixon and Verma 2013) and customers prefer a sequence of experiences that improve over time[12] (and improvement rate may also have an impact: Hsee et al. 1991), the high (or low) points, and, critically, the level of pain (or pleasure) at the end (Redelmeier and Kahneman 1996). Actual duration is relatively unimportant in many service processes; unless an activity is extremely long or extremely short relative to expectations. Increasing the number of events or segments in a service process lengthens how people remember its duration and people can be prompted (primed) to pay attention such that they overestimate duration. Conversely, people fully engaged in a task tend to not observe the passage of time. We will return to many of these psychological insights regarding service processes in the People chapter.

Routines

Discussion of service processes moves us into reflections on less rigid task specifications (e.g., variable work content and timing) structures and here it is useful to take (another) slight detour to engage with the adjacent world of organizational routines. The routines construct, although somewhat ambiguous, has seen widespread 'adoption' in a range of fields such as strategic management (e.g., Eisenhardt and Martin 2000; Teece et al. 1997) and organizational theory (Pentland 1999) and its principal focus is on describing deliberate/emergent order, repetition, interdependence in patterns of action carried out by multiple actors. For this review it is the routines logic as typified by the work of Feldman and Pentland (2003) that offers complementary insights to the idea of process. Organizational routines are presented as the building blocks of organizations and organising. Feldman and Pentland (2003) identified two aspects of organizational routines, the ostensive (what we typically think of as structure, the formal processes and procedures of an operation) and the performative (the specific actions, by specific people, at specific times and places, incorporating a role for the informal, unspoken and emergent: Tranfield and Smith 1998). In other, simpler, words there will be a difference between the 'in principle' and 'in practice' aspects of any routine (process). They should be understood as 'generative' structures, where a common set of inputs can produce a wide variety of different patterns or sequences of events (Fararo and Skvoretz 1984): from the idealized concept of a standardized routine (cf. March and Simon 1958) to a process that seems to generate completely random sequences. Pentland (2003) observes that in "the more common middle", most processes generate "several basic sequences, with occasional variations, exceptions, or shortcuts" (p. 859). Consider how there are often standard work procedures for typical cases but alternative procedures for special cases (Pentland and Rueter 1994). Moreover, in many, many processes (e.g., customer service) there will be multiple ways of accomplishing the same task, what Malone et al. (1999) call 'alternative decompositions', based on variations in requirements, information, employee preferences/skills, etc. Given this additional richness, understanding and measuring variation is much more than simply mapping and measuring. Although undoubtedly powerful as a critical lens on practice (e.g., Brown and Lewis 2011) the underlying theoretical conception of structure as a duality, i.e., the medium and outcome of action, sits uneasily with normative OM and may explain its relatively limited use to date. That said, a more critical realist perspective on the challenges of understanding and analysing routines gives rise to a number of interesting insights. For example, very few processes have a clearly defined start or end point, or are accurately represented by a linear sequence of events, and as such process boundary choices, together with how to represent concurrency, are key parts of practitioner and researcher judgement that are far too often left implicit. Likewise, a reductive process lexicon – such as a narrow set of mapping symbols – can undermine the possibility of detecting genuine process variation.

Concluding comments

What this highlights is how, for all the rich heritage, there remains significant scope for OM scholars to revisit, revise and reinvigorate 'process' as a foundational concept. This might be, as described earlier, in the opportunity for more alternative process theorizing or, more pragmatically, via a greater analytical emphasis, in line with Co-ordination Theory (Malone and Crowston 1994), on non-flow dependencies. In the next chapter we will discuss the planning response (scheduling, prioritizing, etc.) to resource sharing dependencies but (as we will also see in the strategy chapter discussion of operational focus) when OM considers different levels of analysis beyond the single task/process, it also needs to engage with the portfolio dependencies associated with multiple activities combining to produce a single resource (e.g., a patient being treated in a hospital for multiple conditions). Understanding the hierarchy of how different parts of any value proposition fit together or are synchronized, sometimes referred to as the degree of coupling (Orton and Weick 1990; cf. Kellogg and Chase 1995), is critical for successful improvement initiatives. OM – with its manufacturing heritage – has traditionally addressed itself to 'tightly coupled' system but more loosely coupled situations can still exhibit dependencies albeit, as celebrated organizational theorist Karl Weick observed, "suddenly (rather than continuously), occasionally (rather than constantly), negligibly (rather than significantly), and eventually (rather than immediately)" (Weick 1982, p. 380). Equally, future process-centric scholarship might develop and test psychological insights regarding customers *and* employees. Arguably OM has placed insufficient emphasis on the influence of employee attributes on process quality, customer satisfaction, etc. (Yee et al. 2008). Just as the Heskett et al. (1994) service – profit chain concept puts employee satisfaction at the heart of customer satisfaction and business profitability, a greater emphasis on employee concerns (perception of fairness, satisfaction, etc.), organizational culture, empowerment, etc. will likely be critical features of any highly effective service process[13] – especially in knowledge-intensive, flexible, low-volume, etc. settings.

Notes

1 The jeans-clad and paint-spattered Pollock, with his "drip" painting technique was perfectly captured in the photographs and films of German photographer Hans Namuth. They showed how he was using a deliberative, rather than random, paint splashing process and helped transform Pollock into a media superstar. In 1999, Taylor et al. published the results of analysis confirming the poured patterns to be fractal, recurring at increasingly fine magnifications (*Nature*, 422, 399).
2 The painting has featured in films and a Stone Roses song, "Going Down": "she looks like a painting – Jackson Pollock's Number 5 . . .". Their guitarist John Squire created cover artwork for many of the band's releases in a Jackson Pollock style.
3 Other artists, like British painter Bernard Cohen (born 1933), established set processes for 'production' of their work paintings. In his 1963 painting "Inter-Black" for example, Cohen engineered his own spray gun and embarked on a "process of blocking out light" until the canvas was full.
4 Although there is limited explicit engagement with the broader ideas of process theory (Pentland 1999), there is a great deal of potential for further developing these connections.
5 There is some dispute as to whether Smith ever actually visited a pin-making factory or simply took his process descriptions from Diderot's then recently published encyclopaedia.
6 The image of "Liebig's barrel" is used where the shortest stave in a barrel with staves of unequal length limits its capacity.
7 According to Hughes, the "reverse salient" idea was inspired by the military term, referring to a backward bulge in the advancing line of a battle front (e.g., the Verdun salient in WW1).
8 The constraint, or drum, determines the pace of production. The rope is the material release mechanism that releases material to the operation at a pace determined by the constraint. Material release is offset from the constraint schedule by a fixed amount of time, the buffer. Buffers are strategically placed to protect shipping dates and to prevent constraint processes from work starvation (Schragenheim and Ronen 1991).
9 The former head of the department of psychology at the University of Chicago.
10 An assumption that may hold (for the most part) in some heavily machine centric manufacturing systems or modern automated service systems.
11 Shingo was not one of the originators of the concepts but had taught work methods on the P(roduction) Course run by the JMA (Japan Management Association) at Toyota from 1955. He published several books in Japan and was tangentially involved in the

late stages of the development of SMED. Interestingly, on publication of his Toyota book the relationship with the firm ended. He became very well known in the West following his 1981 meeting with Norman Bodek, the American founder of the Productivity Press, who had travelled to Japan to learn about the Toyota Production System.

12 People prefer to have the bad news delivered before the good news, so they prefer a £20 loss followed by a £10 win, to a £10 win then a £20 loss.

13 Of course, such factors are also important in traditional manufacturing settings. In their study of the TQM practices of 'offshore' manufacturing firms (Maquiladora), Jun et al. (2006) validate direct and indirect relationships among top management commitment, HR-focused TQM practices, employee satisfaction, and employee loyalty.

References

Acur, N., & Bititci, U. (2004). A balanced approach to process strategy. *International Journal of Operations and Production Management*, 24(4), 388–408.

Adler, P. S., & Cole, R. E. (1994). NUMMI vs. Uddevalla: Rejoinder. *Sloan Management Review*, 35(2), 37.

Armistead, C., & Machin, S. (1997). Implications of business process management for operations management. *International Journal of Operations and Production Management*, 1(17), 886–898.

Armistead, C., Pritchard, J. P., & Machin, S. (1999). Strategic business process management for organisational effectiveness. *Long Range Planning*, 32(1), 96–106.

Babbage, C. (1864). *Passages from the life of a Philosopher*. 1969 Reprint of 1st ed. M. Kelley, New York.

Benner, M. J., & Tushman, M. L. (2003). Exploitation, exploration, and process management: The productivity dilemma revisited. *Academy of management review*, 28(2), 238–256.

Berggren, C. (1994). Point/counterpoint: NUMMI vs. Uddevalla. *Sloan Management Review*, 35(2), 37.

Bo, Y., Dawande, M., Huh, W. T., Janakiraman, G., & Nagarajan, M. (2018). Determining process capacity: Intractability and efficient special cases. *Manufacturing & Service Operations Management*.

Brown, A. D., & Lewis, M. A. (2011). Identities, discipline and routines. *Organization Studies*, 32(7), 871–895.

Clark, J. R., Huckman, R. S., & Staats, B. R. (2013). Learning from customers: Individual and organizational effects in outsourced radiological services. *Organization Science*, 24(5), 1539–1557.

Carmon, Z., Shanthikumar, J. G., & Carmon, T. F. (1995). A psychological perspective on service segmentation models: The significance of accounting for consumers' perceptions of waiting and service. *Management Science*, 41(11), 1806–1815.

Chase, R. B. (1978). Where does the customer fit in a service operation? *Harvard Business Review*, 56(6), 137–142.

Chase, R. B., & Dasu, S. (2001). Want to perfect your company's service? Use behavioral science. *Harvard Business Review*, 79(6), 78–84.

Collier, D. A., & Meyer, S. M. (1998). A service positioning matrix. *International Journal of Operations & Production Management*, 18(12), 1223–1244.

Cook, L. S., Bowen, D. E., Chase, R. B., Dasu, S., Stewart, D. M., & Tansik, D. A. (2002). Human issues in service design. *Journal of Operations Management*, 20(2), 159–174.

Csikszentmihályi, M. (1990). *Flow: The Psychology of Optimal Experience*. Harper & Row.

Dixon, M., & Verma, R. (2013). Sequence effects in service bundles: Implications for service design and scheduling. *Journal of Operations Management*, 31(3), 138–152.

Eisenhardt, K. M., & Martin, J. A. (2000). Dynamic capabilities: what are they? *Strategic Management Journal, 21*(10–11), 1105–1121.

Fararo, T. J., & Skvoretz, J. (1984). Institutions as production systems. *J. Math. Soc.*, 10, 117–118.

Feldman, M. S., & Pentland, B. T. (2003). Reconceptualizing organizational routines as a source of flexibility and change. *Administrative science quarterly*, 48(1), 94–118.

Fried, Y., & Ferris, G. R. (1987). The validity of the job characteristics model: A review and meta-analysis. *Personnel psychology*, 40(2), 287–322.

Goldratt, E. M., & Cox, J. (1984). *The goal: excellence in manufacturing*. North River Press.

Goldratt, E.M. (1989). *The General Theory of Constraints*, Abraham Goldratt Institute, New Haven, CT.

Golmohammadi, D. (2015). A study of scheduling under the theory of constraints. *International Journal of Production Economics, 165*, 38–50.

Gupta, M., & Snyder, D. (2009). Comparing TOC with MRP and JIT: a literature review. *International Journal of Production Research, 47*(13), 3705–3739.

Gurvich, I., & Van Mieghem, J. A. (2015). Collaboration and multitasking in networks: Architectures, bottlenecks, and capacity. *Manufacturing and Service Operations Management*, 17(1), 16–33.

Gurvich, I., & Van Mieghem, J. A. (2018). Collaboration and prioritization in networks. *Management Science*, 64(5), 2390–2406.

Hammer, M. (2002). Process management and the future of Six Sigma. *MIT Sloan Management Review*, Winter, 26–32.

Hammer, M., & Champy, J. (1993). *Re-Engineering the Corporation: A Manifesto for Business Revolution*. New York, NY: Harper Business.

Heskett, J.L., Sasser, W.E. & Schlesinger, L.A. (1997), *The Service Profit Chain*, Free Press, New York, NY.

Hopp, W. J., Tekin, E., & Van Oyen, M. P. (2004). Benefits of skill chaining in serial production lines with cross-trained workers. *Management Science*, 50(1), 83–98.

Hopp, I., & Liu. (2009). Managing white-collar work. *Production and Operations Management*, 18(1), 1–32.

Hough, J. R., & White, M. A. (2001). Using stories to create change: The object lesson of Frederick Taylor's "pig tale". *Journal of Management*, 27, 585–601.

Hsee, C. K., & Abelson, R. P. (1991). Velocity relation: Satisfaction as a function of the first derivative of outcome over time. *Journal of Personality and Social Psychology*, 60(3), 341.

Huckman, R. S., & Zinner, D. E. (2008). Does focus improve operational performance? Lessons from the management of clinical trials. *Strategic Management Journal*, 29(2), 173–193.

Johns, T., Laubscher, R. J., & Malone, T. W. (2011). The age of hyper specialization. *Harvard Business Review*, 89(7–8), 56.

Jun, M., Cai, S., & Shin, H. (2006). TQM practice in maquiladora: Antecedents of employee satisfaction and loyalty. *Journal of Operations Management*, 24(6), 791–812.

KC, D. S., & Terwiesch, C. (2009). Impact of workload on service time and patient safety: An econometric analysis of hospital operations. *Management Science*, 55(9), 1486–1498.

KC, D. S., & Terwiesch, C. (2011). The effects of focus on performance: Evidence from California hospitals. *Management Science*, 57(11), 1897–1912.

Kellogg, D. L., & Chase, R. B. (1995). Constructing an empirically derived measure for customer contact. *Management Science*, 41(11), 1734–1749.

Linderman, K., Schroeder, R. G., Zaheer, S., & Choo, A. S. (2003). Six Sigma: A goal theoretic perspective. *Journal of Operations Management*, 21, 193–203.

Llewellyn, N., & Armistead, C. (2000). Business process management: Exploring social capital within processes. *International Journal of Service Industry Management*, 11(3), 225–243.

Locke, E. (1982). The ideas of Frederick Taylor: an evaluation. *Academy of Management Review*, 7, 14–24.

Love, P. E. D., Gunasekeran, A., & Li, H. (1998). Putting an engine into re-engineering: Toward a process-oriented organisation. *International Journal of Operations and Production Management*, 18(9/10), 937–949.

MacIntosh, R. (2003). BPR: Alive and well in the public sector. *International Journal of Operations and Production Management*, 23, 327–344.

Malone, T. W., & Crowston, K. (1994). The interdisciplinary study of coordination. *ACM Computing Surveys (CSUR)*, 26(1), 87–119.

Malone, T. W., Crowston, K., Lee, J., Pentland, B., Dellarocas, C., Wyner, G., ... & Klein, M. (1999). Tools for inventing organizations: Toward a handbook of organizational processes. *Management Science*, 45(3), 425–443.

March, J. G., & Simon, H. A. (1958). *Organizations*, Wiley, New York.

Melan, E. (1989). Process management: A unifying framework. *National Productivity Review*, 8, 395–406.

Nelson, L. D., & Meyvis, T. (2008). Interrupted consumption: Adaptation and the disruption of hedonic experience. *Journal of Marketing Research*, 45(6), 654–64.

Oldham, G. R., & Fried, Y. (2016). Job design research and theory: Past, present and future. *Organizational Behavior and Human Decision Processes*, 136, 20–35.

Ortega, J. (2001). Job rotation as a learning mechanism. *Management Science*, 47, 1361–1370.

Orton, J. D., & Weick, K. E. (1990). Loosely coupled systems: A reconceptualization. *Academy of Management Review*, 15(2), 203–223.

Pentland, B. T. (1999). Building process theory with narrative: From description to explanation. *Academy of Management Review*, 24(4).

Pentland, B. T. (2003). Sequential variety in work processes. *Organization Science*, 14(5), 528–540.

Pentland, B. T., & Feldman, M. S. (2008). Designing routines: On the folly of designing artifacts, while hoping for patterns of action. *Information and Organization*, 18(4), 235–250.

Pentland, B. T., & Rueter, H. (1994). Organisational Routines as Grammars of Action, *Administrative Sciences Quarterly*, 39.

Poppendieck, M., & Poppendieck, T. (2006). *Implementing Lean Software Development: From Concept to Cash*. Addison-Wesley.

Rahman, S. U. (1998). Theory of constraints: a review of the philosophy and its applications. International *Journal of Operations & Production Management*, 18(4), 336–355.

Redelmeier, D. A., & Kahneman, D. (1996). Patients' memories of painful medical treatments: Real-time and retrospective evaluations of two minimally invasive procedures. *Pain*, 66(1), 3–8.

Reijers, H. A., & Liman Mansar, S. (2004). Best practices in business process redesign: An overview and qualitative evaluation of successful redesign heuristics. *Omega: The International Journal of Management Science*, 33, 283–306.

Rosen, L., & Samuel, A. (2015). Conquering digital distraction. *Harvard Business Review*, 93(6), 110–113.

Sampson, S. E., & Froehle, C. M. (2006). Foundations and implications of a proposed unified services theory. *Production and Operations Management*, 15(2), 329–343.

Schmenner, R. W., & Swink, M. L. (1998). On theory in operations management. *Journal of Operations Management*, 17(1), 97–113.

Schragenheim, E., & Ronen, B. (1991). Buffer management: a diagnostic tool for production control. *Production and Inventory Management Journal*, 32(2), 74–79.

Schultz, K. L., McClain, J. O., & Thomas, L. J. (2003). Overcoming the dark side of worker flexibility. *Journal of Operations Management*, 21(1), 81–92.

Skinner, W. (1974). The focused factory. *Harvard Bus. Rev.*, May/June, 113–121.

Smart, P. A., Maddern, H., & Maull, R. S. (2009). Understanding business process management: Implications for theory and practice. *British Journal of Management*, 20(4), 491–507.

Smith, A. (1776). *An inquiry into the nature and causes of the wealth of nations: Volume One*. London: printed for W. Strahan; and T. Cadell, 1776.

Staats, B. R., & Gino, F. (2012). Specialization and variety in repetitive tasks: Evidence from a Japanese bank. *Management Sci.*, 58(6), 1141–1159.

Stuart, I., McCutcheon, D., Handfield, R., McLachlin, R., & Samson, D. (2002). Effective case research in operations management: A process perspective. *Journal of Operations Management*, 20, 419–433.

Taylor, F. W. (1911). *The principles of scientific management*. New York, 202.

Teece, D. J., Pisano, G., & Shuen, A. (1997). Dynamic capabilities and strategic management. *Strategic Management Journal*, 18(7), 509–533.

Terzioski, M., Fitzpatrick, P., & O'Neil, P. (2003). Successful predictors of Business Process Reengineering (BPR) in financial services. *International Journal of Production Economics*, 84, 35–50.

Thürer, M., Stevenson, M., Silva, C., & Qu, T. (2017). Drum-buffer-rope and workload control in high-variety flow and job shops with bottlenecks: An assessment by simulation. *International Journal of Production Economics*, 188, 116–127.

Tranfield, D., & Smith, S. (1998). The strategic regeneration of manufacturing by changing routines. *International Journal of Operations & Production Management*, 18(2), 114–129.

Tsikriktsis, N. (2007). The effect of operational performance and focus on profitability: A longitudinal study of the U.S. airline industry. *Manufacturing and Service Operations Management*, 9(4), 506–517.

Tucker, A. L., Nembhard, I. M., & Edmondson, A. C. (2007). Implementing new practices: An empirical study of organizational learning in hospital intensive care units. *Management Sci.*, 53(6), 894–907.

Walker, C. R., & Guest, R. H. (1952). *The man on the assembly line*. Cambridge, MA, US: Harvard University Press.

Watson, K. J., Blackstone, J. H., & Gardiner, S. C. (2007). The evolution of a management philosophy: The theory of constraints. *Journal of Operations Management*, 25(2), 387–402.

Weick, K. E. (1982). Management of Organizational Change Among Loosely Coupled Elements. Reprinted in: Weick, KE (2001). *Making Sense of the Organization*, Oxford, UK (Blackwell).

Womack, J. P., & Jones, D. T. (1996). Beyond Toyota: how to root out waste and pursue perfection. *Harvard Business Review*, 74(5), 140–158.

Yee, R. W., Yeung, A. C., & Cheng, T. E. (2008). The impact of employee satisfaction on quality and profitability in high-contact service industries. *Journal of Operations Management*, 26(5), 651–668.

3 Planning and control

The Sampling Officials (De Staalmeesters), completed by Rembrandt in 1662, has been described as his last great collective portrait. It hangs in the Rijksmuseum in Amsterdam and this extraordinary painting marks the transition to our second theme. It shows a group of inspectors, drapers who had been elected to carry out inspections three times a week, assessing a length of fabric (the Dutch word *staal* means 'sample'). The inspectors pressed the seals of their city and guild into slugs of lead that were attached to record the results of the inspection (four seals being the best and one seal the lowest quality). The challenge of planning and control (of quality, etc.) is arguably one of the foundational themes in contemporary OM. Although the focus here is on more managerial discussions,[1] even this review highlights that this is an area where the boundary between OM and OR (and mathematics, computer science, etc.) becomes very blurred.

Planning

Having spent a whole chapter discussing process and flow as defining concepts for OM, it should come as no surprise that related planning tasks such as 'what work should be done in what order' and 'who should do it?' are a consequentially fundamental concern. Revisiting our historical theme, determining when a resource becomes available, which task that resource should do next, who should complete the work, etc. will be as old as task specialization. Although little is actually known of Imhotep, chancellor to the pharaoh Djoser, he is widely discussed as the probable architect of the step pyramid at Saqqara in Egypt (constructed between 2630–2611 BC). The organizational implications of such a large (62m tall with a base of 109m × 125m) and complex (clad in polished white limestone) structure are staggering. Processes would have been far more labour-intensive than previous mud-brick experience and have involved a more distant supply chain, suggesting that the royal government had a significant level of control over material and human resources. Despite this ancient legacy, it is not until the work of Henry Gantt (a one-time colleague of FW Taylor) that we have the first[2] systematic attempt to advance general principles of scheduling.

Over time, increasingly sophisticated analytical techniques have been applied to the challenge. Linear programming (i.e., optimizing a linear objective function) was first applied to production planning problems in the 1940s and, after George Dantzig (see 1982 article) 'invented[3]' the simplex method, this extremely powerful technique has been applied to ever more operational applications. Throughout the 1950s, in many ways a golden era for analytical OM (integrating OR concepts that had themselves been spurred on by the demands of global conflict), a number of mathematical solutions for sequencing problems were developed.[4] As an illustration it is instructive to take a moment to consider the seminal Johnson's rule (1954). Given a set of jobs to be processed by two work centres, where no machine can process more than one job at any time; and the two work centres are separated by an (unlikely) infinite capacity waiting room. Johnson's rule, to minimize the total time required to complete all work, essentially says: (1) select the job with the shortest activity time. If that activity time is for the first work machine, then schedule the job first. (2) If that activity time is for the second work centre then schedule the job last. (3) Eliminate the shortest job from further consideration. (4) Repeat steps 2 and 3, until all jobs have been scheduled. Many of these problems/solutions are still being researched today (e.g., Tellache and Boudhar 2017). Ultimately, however engaging these problems and elegant the solutions, solving more complex practical problems required a different approach. For example, branch-and-bound algorithms emerged in the 1960s (Land and Doig 1960) to search through successive configurations (or states) of a problem,[5] with the intention of efficiently finding a goal state with a desired property (e.g., minimum production time). The name "branch and bound" first appeared in the Little et al. (1963) application to the travelling salesman problem (i.e., given a list of destinations and the distances between each pair of destinations, what is the shortest possible route that visits each one and returns to the origin?). Recently, scheduling research has included optimization of a broader range of performance objectives, including energy efficiency and other sustainability concerns (e.g., Giret et al. 2015).

Having spent a whole chapter discussing process as a foundational concept, it should come as no surprise that allocating workload, especially when managing assembly lines (flow-line production systems with, typically, high capital investment requirements), has produced a significant scholarly OM response. There is a body of 'classic' configuration, assignment of tasks to workstations, work (e.g., Salveson 1955; Baybars 1986), that has generated different solutions contingent on different objectives – maximizing line efficiency, minimizing the number of stations for a given cycle time, minimizing cycle time for a given number of stations, etc. (Scholl and Becker 2006) – and over the last 50+ years various additional constraints, parallel stations, lines, etc. (Scholl and Becker 2006; Boysen et al. 2007) have also been addressed. Today, as previously 'fixed' machines have, via automation, become much more flexible with negligible setup times/costs, the line balancing problem has persisted and remains a subject of significant research interest. The increasing availability of ever more powerful computing power has been transformative for complex scheduling, not just for the greater complexity of tasks that can be attempted, but for the speed with which decent solutions can be obtained. Practitioners generally need solutions in a reasonable amount of time.

Although the high-volume, tightly controlled assembly line is perhaps the archetype for industrial efficiency, OM addresses many different types of operating systems, from the two-machine job shop of Johnson's rule to a wide range of higher variety, lower volume systems that place a premium on flexibility *and* lower cost. One particularly interesting, decentralized, approach to production planning is the so-called 'bucket brigade' where workers walk to adjacent stations to continue work on an item. The original work by Bartholdi and Eisenstein (1996) was derived from analysis of the "Toyota Sewn Products Management System" (TSS) for use in the manufacture of many types of sewn products but the approach has also been applied in many other settings, including phone packing and assembly of automotive electrical harnesses (Bartholdi and Eisenstein 2005). Although seemingly counter-intuitive, each worker follows a simple rule: continue working on a product along the line until either your colleague downstream takes over your work or you finish your work at the end of the line; then you walk back to get more work, either from your colleague upstream or from a buffer at the start of the line. Bartholdi and Eisenstein (1996) show (assuming workers have deterministic, finite work velocity and an infinite walk-back velocity) that if the workers are sequenced from slowest to fastest then a bucket brigade will self-balance and workers will repeatedly work on a fixed segment of the line. Furthermore, if the work content is continuously and uniformly distributed along the line, then the long-run average throughput will achieve the maximum possible value for the system. There have been numerous conceptual extensions of the original bucket brigade model (e.g., Armbruster et al. (2007), Webster et al. (2012), Lim and Wu (2014), etc.) but most interestingly, unlike many other line balancing solutions, bucket brigades have proved to be effective and attractive for practitioners. The approach is appealing because: (1) The rule is easy for workers to follow; (2) There is no requirement for work balance computation; and (3) It balances workload for workers subject to variability, and 'spontaneously' adapts to disruptions. These 'self-organizing' properties have been popularized as a bio-mimetic system, emulating the behaviour of social insects. Specifically, just as there are many tasks to be performed within an ant colony, including nest building, nest defence, foraging, food storage, queen care, brood care and so on. It is critical that ants get the work-allocation balance right. Biologists have studied such questions in detail and found that the social insects can develop near optimal solutions to resource allocation problems (Wilson and Hölldobler 2009).

Service planning

A key variant of the planning challenge is the provision of the requisite number of appropriately qualified human resources (people!) at the specified time at the appropriate (minimum?) cost. Although the field of workforce planning is a vast subject with its own heritage (e.g., Heneman and Sandver 1977; Price et al. 1980) it is worth introducing to our narrative at this point. Intriguingly, just as telephony systems had a significant impact on our understanding of queues (Palm 1953), etc. – the emergence of large-scale call centres,[6] with their associated resource 'acquisition' and 'deployment' challenges (e.g., demand forecasting, how large a pool of agents to hire, with what skills, at what times, with what shift pattern, on what contractual basis, how to do real-time call routing, the balance of core service v. cross-selling, employee turnover and absenteeism levels, etc.) have provided fertile ground for analytical OM to more fully engage with service systems (e.g., Avramidis et al. 2004; Akşin et al. 2007; Aldor-Noiman et al. 2009). It is also a setting where there is a great deal of overlap between the analytical representations of the system and the managerial tools used to manage them. Consider a call centre as a simple queuing system (Gans et al. 2003; Armony et al. 2009) with a certain number of lines connected to a certain number of seats/agents. If an agent is free an incoming call is put immediately into service or, if the agents are all busy, the arriving call waits in a queue for an agent to be available on a first come, first-served basis. Some callers will be impatient and abandon. Once a call is completed the system/agent becomes available for the next call. Call centre managers need to adjust characteristics of the system (e.g., number of agents, scripting, etc.), and their decisions are frequently informed by queueing models (e.g., the M/M/N or Erlang C[7]) based on statistics for arrival, abandonment and service times, etc.

Ultimately, just as technologies brought the modern call centre into being (e.g., Rockwell International patented its Galaxy Automatic Call Distributor (GACD) in 1973), so other technologies have changed the operating mix (e.g., adding in interactive voice response (IVR) technology creates a more complex process flow), and newer innovations (speech recognition, AI, etc.) will continue to do so; however, this remains fertile ground for service OM scholars.

Inventory

In 1913, when Ford W. Harris[8] published his 3-page article asking "How many parts to make at once" it seems unlikely he could have imagined that, more than 100 years later, it would still be the subject of extensive OM discussion and research (Erlenkotter 1990). Even today, industrial engineering and business students study the Economic Order Quantity (EOQ) formula, sometimes as part of specific assessment of inventory systems, or more broadly as a good illustration of the concept of cost trade-offs. The model indicates order quantities for items, so as to minimize associated costs (balancing fixed costs against carrying costs is the basis for arriving at the economic order quantity).

The original model made some significant assumptions – continuous demand, constant inventory usage rate and no order or storage quantity constraints, instantaneous replenishment, no shortages and invariant time and quantity costs – that were later relaxed as variants of the basic model were developed. The seminal Wagner-Whitin solution (1958) for example, allows for product demand varying over time. They generated an algorithm for finding the optimal solution by dynamic programming but, especially given the constraints of contemporary computing, the complexity of this method subsequently led many researchers to develop approximate heuristics for the problem. Whitin was also one of the first scholars to adapt the newsvendor model to examine how market and operational problems interact. In this elegant and intuitively appealing model, a decision-maker facing demand for a product that becomes obsolete must decide how many units of the product to stock in order to maximize expected profit. The first modern formulation[9] of the (originally "newsboy") problem can be found in an *Econometrica* paper by Arrow et al. (1951). The optimal solution to this problem is characterized by a balance between the expected cost of under-stocking and the expected cost of overstocking. Whitin (1955) established a sequential procedure for determining first the optimal stocking quantity as a function of price and then the corresponding optimal price. Mills (1959) refined the formulation in a way that better emphasizes the integration of marketing and operations decisions by explicitly specifying mean demand as a function of the selling price (see also Petruzzi and Dada 1999, etc.). Today, newsvendor models play a pivotal role in the literature on stochastic inventory theory (Chen et al. 2016).

To cope with the inventory challenge that has escalated under variety driving strategies such as mass customization (Su et al. 2005), alongside sophisticated forecasting and planning techniques, many firms design multiple variants of a product such that they can begin production using common sub-assemblies or modules and only later differentiate into specific variants. Famously, HP adopted such a strategy for its DeskJet printers, starting production on one common product, and then later, at the distribution centre, localizing the printer for individual geographic markets (Kopczak and Lee 2004). This is not a new concept – the Venice Arsenale stored vessel sub-assemblies on land to allow them to rapidly respond to demand for ships. In addition to deciding where in a process/supply chain to locate the so-called decoupling or postponement point (Lee and Tang 1997), there is also the question of where to hold inventory in such a system (Van der Rhee et al. 2017).

Service inventory

Queuing Theory is central to the concept of service inventory. Dating back to 1909, when Agner Krarup Erlang (1878–1929) published his pioneering work on telephone traffic, the simplest models describe customers arriving at a server according to a Poisson process (rate λ) and served by a server (rate μ). If the server is idle when a customer arrives, the service starts immediately, else the customer stays in a queue.[10] When $\lambda \geq \mu$, the system explodes in the long run, that is, queues tend to grow with limit. More complicated models can be studied by modifying assumptions about arrival and service times or by assuming that customers may have to go through more than one server. In most of these models, customers are essentially passive 'inventory' and make no strategic decisions (we revisit the more behavioural character of 'real' queues in the next chapter). We have already discussed how a call centre might be represented as a queue and how variants of the newsvendor model combine capacity planning and control with pricing/ demand management, but many operations face distinct managerial challenges with respect to the time-bound value or perishability of service "inventory" (airline seats, etc.). What is often designated as yield management – "sell[ing] the right inventory unit to the right type of customer, at the right time and at the right price" (Kimes 1989) – has become critical to maximization of revenue/profit. Some of the earliest scientific approaches to yield planning emerged in airline operations. From early experiments with controlled overbooking (using probability distributions of number of passengers who were no-shows/go-shows for flights), in the early 1970s, some airlines began offering restricted discount fare products that mixed discount and higher fare passengers in the same aircraft. BOAC (now British Airways) offered *early bird* bookings that charged lower fares to passengers who booked at least 21 days in advance of flight departure. The advantages were clear, potential revenue from seats that would otherwise have been empty; but it also created the analytical problem of determining the number of seats that should be protected for late booking full fare passengers (too few and they miss out on full fare passengers; too many, flights depart with empty seats). Effective control of discount seats required detailed tracking of booking histories, expansion of information system capabilities and careful research and development of seat inventory control rules. Littlewood (1972) of BOAC proposed that discount fare bookings should be accepted as long as their revenue value exceeded the expected revenue of future full fare bookings (Littlewood's rule). This simple, two fare, seat inventory control rule marked the beginning of what came to be called yield, later revenue management. Today, no airline could trade without a revenue management capability. Dynamic pricing allows for profit maximization through market segmentation – a functionality rendered more critical (and more challenging) with the emergence of online travel agents and intense competition from low-cost carriers (Alderighi et al. 2015). The benefits of revenue management have led to its adoption in many other service industries, including mobile telephony (customers 'acquired' with discounted plans and then retained at higher price points), car rental (checking comparative rates, demand scenarios, etc.) and hotels (key operating indicators such as Occupancy Rate (OR), Average Daily Rate (ADR) and Revenue per Available Room (RevPAR) are tracked using third-party data sources to follow competitor set averages in demand and price).

Control

The Rembrandt painting reminds us that ideas of quality control and assurance have a very long history, but the last century has seen an avalanche of analytical and conceptual development in this core area of OM. Think about the QA department at AT&T Bell Laboratories during the first half of the twentieth century; it must have been an extraordinary place, home to various statistical luminaries, including Walter A. Shewhart,[11] Harold Dodge[12] and Harry Romig,[13] whose work – again accelerated by the exigencies of war – would transform industrial practice. Together with others they worked on the basic concepts that would become the core of modern quality control, bringing statistical rigour to both sampling and process control. Although often considered under the same quality control rubric, these are of course fundamentally different approaches. Sampling is not per se about improving underlying process but determining quality risk in those circumstances where 100% testing is problematic (e.g., Dodge and Romig applied acceptance sampling to bullets, the ultimate 'one shot' product); "producer's risk" (the probability of incorrectly rejecting a good batch) and "consumer's risk" (the probability of incorrectly accepting a bad batch). SPC on the other hand is a tool that is (part of) a systematic mechanism for process control and improvement. As discussed in chapter 2, all processes have a degree of 'instability'; that is, they have multiple consistent and special sources of variation. Most are minor and can (potentially) be ignored, but if assignable sources of variation are detected, they can (potentially) be removed, making a process more "stable" – its variation remaining within known limits – at least, until another assignable source of variation occurs! The quality mechanism is straightforward; when a process triggers control chart 'detection rules', improvement activities[14] should be performed to identify the source of the excessive variation.

Beyond setting up specific measures and identifying relevant improvement mechanisms, the broader managerial challenge is how to develop a more holistic approach to improvement and change. The challenge of monitoring multiple processes has led to the use of meta-metrics to help prioritizing which processes are most in need of corrective action (e.g., in addition to 'simple' Cp process capability metrics, Ramirez and Runger (2006) highlight three key measures: the Stability Ratio comparing long-term/short-term variability, ANOVA tests to compare within/between-subgroup variation, and the Instability Ratio which compares the number of subgroups with violations of the 'Western Electric rules'[15] to the total number of subgroups). These ideas have become so deeply ingrained in industrial practice that they feature infrequently in OM scholarship. That said, given there are many applications where simultaneous monitoring/control of two or more related quality characteristics is necessary, treating them as independent can be very misleading. Consequently, although not a novel concern (it was first described by Hotelling (1947) in his pioneering bombsights paper) there have been some interesting developments in dealing with multivariate process control techniques and autocorrelated (i.e., for many processes, observations are not independent, where the current value provides no indication of the next value, but rather dependent or autocorrelated) data sets (e.g., Lowry and Montgomery 1995; Runger 1996; Lu 1998; Bersimis et al. 2007, etc.).

From TQM to Six Sigma

Over the last 30+ years quality has gone in and out of fashion as a high-profile practitioner – and scholarly – concern. The modern Six Sigma movement for example, originated at Motorola in about 1987[16] – followed by Allied Signal and then the very high-profile implementation of Six at General Electric beginning in 1995 – as a way for the firm to convey its ambitious quality goal of 3.4 DPMO[17] (i.e., process variability is ±6σ from the mean, they also assumed that the process mean could, under disturbances, shift by as much as 1.5 S.D. off the target) that required aggressive improvement efforts (Folaron 2003). Scholars (and OM scholars in particular) were relatively late to a structured exploration of 6σ (Hahn et al. 1999; Schroeder et al. 2008) in part because it was widely characterized as a repackaging of old(er) quality management approaches (cf. Cole 1999). Identifying the truly distinctive aspects of Six Sigma is non-trivial. After all, balancing the technical and social aspects of quality practices was also central to Deming's ideas on quality. He emphasized the pivotal role of variability, famously theorizing that special causes are typically attributable to quickly identifiable factors, common causes remain when special causes have been eliminated but also understood the organizational factors (e.g., it is 'workers' who typically recognize common causes but only managers have the authority to change things). The key point of distinction is probably the specific emphasis placed on novel organizational structures. Schroeder et al. (2008, p. 540) define it as "an organized, parallel-meso structure used to reduce variation in organizational processes by employing improvement specialists, a structured method, and customer-oriented performance metrics with the aim of achieving strategic objectives". Although multiple variants are observed in practice, it typically involves the creation of an authority structure (yellow, green, black, master black, etc.) together with significant training efforts (training costs as high as $50,000 per worker have been reported) on a structured problem-solving method (DMAIC). Like TQM before it, observers of Six Sigma have identified success and failure stories but Swink and Jacobs (2012) found, in a study of 214 adopting firms, an average 4-year post-adoption increase in abnormal ROA of 0.83% and Jacobs et al. (2015) found that late adopters of Six Sigma fare better, especially – unsurprisingly! – if they are large and financially healthy and in industries with low technological velocity and/or B2B market orientation. To reconnect this to our earlier discuss of routines/process, OM consideration of the diffusion of administrative innovations has often neglected endogenous (ostensive/performative) and exogenous (e.g., specific needs and contexts: Strang and Kim 2004) variation over time. Differences in Six Sigma adoption have included differential usage of Black Belt roles, different performance metrics (e.g., customer satisfaction versus dollar savings), and, perhaps most interestingly from an OM perspective, combinations with other administrative innovations such as Lean and Agile methods.

Lean production: integrating planning and control?

The description and dissemination of 'lean'[18] is arguably the most significant contemporary contribution to, and made by, the OM field. It not only challenged the logic of mass production in its originating setting, the automotive industry, but its widely accepted link to superior performance (e.g., Krafcik 1988; Shah and Ward 2003) has moved global operations practice. The Lean Production (LP) model relates manufacturing performance advantage to adherence to key principles (Womack et al. 1990; Womack and Jones 1996) that act to integrate and refine many of the process and planning/control issues discussed so far. The first, process-focused, principle, to improve the flow of material and information across business functions, is challenging but seemingly intuitive and has been widely discussed in this work already. The second, planning-focused, principle is more counter-intuitive:[19] an emphasis on customer *pull* rather than organization *push*, prioritizing WIP reduction over capacity utilization (compare this with a classic line balance approach) enabled by (and/or necessitate) production smoothing ('heijunka'), quick setup times and stages closely inter-connected by kanbans. The third, control-focused, principle, a commitment to continuous improvement enabled by people development has today become almost axiomatic.

Post-1945 Japanese industrial development (especially, but not exclusively, in the automotive industry) was obviously following a different trajectory (Sugimori et al. 1977), most clearly embodied in the Toyota Production System, but it was not isolated from global practice. In the immediate post-war period it was small (in 1950, Japan as a whole was producing, annually, an output equivalent to less than 3 days' of US car production), and *Japanese-made* was often a synonym for 'cheap' and 'poor quality'. Yet, over time, more and more Japanese brands, especially electronic and automotive firms, were growing aggressively and taking more and more market share from established 'Western' firms. It is also ironic that despite an apparent lack of interest in the details of this transformation, at least until the oil price shock of 1973, it was helped along the way by Japanese engagement with US and European practice. During the US occupation of Japan (1945–1952) for example, the General HQ of the Allied occupation ordered vacuum tubes from Tokyo Shibaura Engineering (Toshiba), asking to see the 'control charts' from the manufacturing process. According to Eizaburo Nishibori,[20] no-one at Toshiba knew what this was. Soon after, GHQ officers began giving – initially poorly attended – lectures to their Japanese vendors, using QC books obtained from their Washington D.C. office. The GHQ also arranged Deming's first visit to Japan. The Japanese government was about to conduct its first post-war national census but the cabinet level statisticians resisted Deming's ideas for sampling and opted for a 100% survey. Government officials may not have appreciated his advice but Japanese industry leaders asked him to return and teach them QC and consequently, in 1950 Deming introduced SQC at his historic Mt. Hakone Conference centre talk.[21] Attended by senior industrial managers, representing an estimated 75% of industrial capital base of Japan at that time, Deming stressed the importance of using statistical analysis, enabled by management, in addressing both product quality and market awareness:

> You, Japan's skillful technicians, can manufacturer items that businessmen of American and the rest of the world cannot. You don't know whether the things you want to sell are what Americans want to buy, but you know the way to find this out. That method is statistical research in the realms of manufacture and market surveying.

Similarly, when Eiji Toyoda became managing director of Toyota's manufacturing arm he was sent to the United States to study American manufacturing methods. Holweg (2007) also notes that a pre-war Toyota delegation "had visited the Focke-Wulff aircraft works in Germany, where they observed the 'Produktionstakt' concept, which later developed into what we now know as 'takt time'" (p. 421). Ultimately, Toyota found ways to combine the advantages of small-batch production with economies of scale but this process took many years – hence the central emphasis on individual and systemic learning in the reification of the LP model: "Toyota-style system has been neither purely original nor totally imitative. It is essentially a hybrid" (Fujimoto 1999, p. 50). Over time, key lessons from TPS began to merge into the construct we know today as lean production (LP). Holweg (2007) provides an excellent summary of the co-evolution of Lean theory and practice and his reflections reinforce this notion that production concepts continue to develop and change. Although the moment of 'peak lean production' may have passed, organizations continue to wrestle with profound planning and control challenges and, consequently, OM still needs to engage with contemporary operational practice. Miyake (2006) and Yin et al. (2017) for example highlight the emergence of another form of Japanese production system – "seru seisan" (*seru* means cell, and *seisan* means production) – as a response to market requirements for smaller volumes and higher variety. This approach is widely used but especially in the electronics industry, where product size and weight (cf. automobiles) mean that manual operation and transport is easier. In sum, a *Seru Seisan* organization replaces long assembly lines with many short ones. Once again, this approach did not emerge fully formed; cellular manufacturing has long been classified as a critical subsection of JIT manufacturing but, like TPS, it is derived from much older principles still. In this case group technology (e.g., Flanders[22] 1925; Mitrofanov 1933 (tr. 1959); Hyer and Wemmerlov 1984). Grouping parts with similar manufacturing characteristics into families reduces time spent on setups, something that is particularly significant in lower volume manufacturing. A cell is constructed by consolidating only the processes required to create a specific output, such as a particular part, thus eliminating extraneous steps. The (often U-shaped) cellular structure allows for greater visibility of all parts of the process but typically there has been a significant emphasis on automation and the separation of machine-work and operator-work so that machines work independently as much as possible. The *Seru Seisan* system is a low-automation system; in a *Seru*, movable workstations, light equipment and continuously cross-trained workers allow for rapid re-configurations for several dedicated product types. All of the equipment is grouped by the similarities of products rather than the function of machines (Villa and Taurino 2013).

Concluding comments

Ultimately, it is only by viewing production systems (like LP, Seru, etc.) as evolving and integrated concepts that it is possible to reconcile the dynamic overlap among their various components (Shah and Ward 2007). No integrated approach to planning and control, including LP, can be viewed as "a singular concept" and any overly reductive perspective (i.e., it's Kanban or quality circles or Andon cords, or A3 plans, etc.) however attractive it may be to practitioners ('this is the answer') and scholars ('this problem can be solved') is ultimately misleading. Any insightful discussion must consider internal and external (i.e., supplier and customer) factors and, critically, people and their behaviour.

Notes

1 Project scheduling is closely related to this discussion but is also outside the scope of the text.

2 Another method of representing process interdependencies was invented, but only published in Polish, in 1896 by Karol Adamiecki (see Marsh 1975 for a fascinating overview of his work on the Harmonogram).

3 Arguably, it was invented/discovered three times, independently, between 1939 and 1947. The first time by L. V. Kantorovich, a Soviet citizen, the second was by Dutchman T. C. Koopmans and the third time by G. B. Dantzig.

4 Equally during this fertile period, the earliest due date (EDD) rule for minimizing maximum lateness, and the shortest processing time (SPT) rule for minimizing average flow time (and the ratio variant for minimizing weighted flow time).

5 The set of possible solutions is thought of as forming a rooted tree. The algorithm explores branches (i.e., subsets of the solution set) of this tree. Before enumerating candidate solutions in the branch, it is checked against upper and lower estimated bounds on the optimal solution and is discarded if it cannot produce a better solution than the best one found so far by the algorithm.

6 The Birmingham Press and Mail (UK) installed Private Automated Business Exchanges (PABX), with rows of agents handling customer contacts, in the late 1960s. Throughout the 1970s, call centres were used for telephone sales, airline reservations and banking systems. During the 1990s, they expanded and increasingly became (multi-channel, digitally enabled) contact centres. They were also at the epicentre of the outsourcing phenomena as third-party providers offered "pay per use" services.

7 One of Erlang's foundational formulae for teletraffic engineering and queueing theory. Erlang-C as a simplified model (e.g., it takes no account of services that require multiple calls) gives the probability that a new call will need to wait in a queue (nb. the formula may fail to hold when congestion is high and unsuccessful traffic repeatedly re-dial).

8 Harris was a self-taught engineer. He published 70+ articles, held some 50 patents and retired from engineering to "read the law". He was admitted to the California bar and became a successful patent lawyer (Roach 2005).

9 The newsvendor problem has a rich history that has been traced back to the economist Edgeworth (1888), who applied a variant to a bank cash-flow problem.

10 This model is expressed as M/M/1, to indicate that both arrival and service times are Markovian (memoryless) and there is only one server.

11 In 1918, after his PhD in Physics, Shewhart joined the Western Electric Co. Inspection Engineering Department at the Hawthorne Works (more on this celebrated plant later). On May 16, 1924 Shewhart prepared a 1-page memo, presenting a proto-control chart and explaining all of the essential principles of statistical process quality control.

12 During WWII, Dodge served as consultant to the Secretary of War. He was also chairman of the American Standards Association and after retiring from Bell Labs became a professor of applied mathematical statistics at Rutgers.

13 Romig was closely associated with Dodge; their best-known collaboration the Dodge-Romig sampling tables. But they also developed sampling plans (with producer and consumer risks) and operating characteristics for sampling plans.

14 This is where SPC is a necessary but not sufficient part of quality control. Once an assignable variation is identified, an improvement system invokes a whole range of other analytical tools (including Ishikawa diagrams, experiments, Pareto charts, etc.)

and process interventions (training, error-proofing/poke yoke, etc.). This holistic response is what lies behind the Total Quality Management designation.

15 The 'rules' used for detecting out-of-control or non-random conditions on control charts, using the locations of observations relative to control chart control limits (typically at ±3σ) and centreline. They were published in a 1956 handbook, that became a standard text, by the manufacturing division of the Western Electric Company.

16 From the early 1980s, after many observers documented major quality gaps between US and Japanese companies, the first boom market emerged for quality-related advice and guidance. W. Edwards Deming became a celebrity and – as an illustration of the market for such advice – by the end of the 1980s managers at the (in)famous US utility company Florida Power and Light (the first non-Japanese winner of the prestigious Deming quality prize) estimated that 90% of the Fortune 100 companies had attended their monthly seminars. Indeed, to cope with the demand, FPL set a subsidiary consulting operation, Qualtec.

17 Defects Per Million Opportunities. It is used (cf. parts per million, PPM, defective) to indicate the possibility that a unit under inspection may have multiple defects of the same type or multiple types of defects.

18 The term lean is typically attributed to John Krafcik, the first American engineer to be hired by NUMMI (the GM/Toyota JV) and subsequently key player with Womack et al., in the assembly plant studies that would eventually become MIT International Motor Vehicle Program (IMVP). It is difficult today to imagine the impact of this work but, to give a sense of it, an early paper showed that NUMMI achieved, in its first year, 50% higher productivity levels and the best quality within GM's entire US operation. As noted by Holweg (2007), this terminology had its own history. Haruo Shimada from Keio University (and visiting at the Sloan School) studied US auto transplants using a benchmarking index which classified companies from 'fragile' to 'robust' or 'buffered'. This terminology that was initially used by IMVP researchers, but 'fragile' was later changed to the more positive sounding 'lean'.

19 Interestingly, although 'traditional' push planning techniques (as embodied in MRP systems, etc.) and JIT/LP are often caricatured as contradictory philosophies of production, several authors have pointed out the overlaps and similarities between both the concept and practical intent of these different control techniques. Spearman and Zazanis (1992) for instance, extend these comparisons by introducing the CONWIP analytical model, a production system with a constant level of WIP and a hybrid of push and pull control (Spearman et al. 1990).

20 Eizaburo Nishibori (1903–1989) was a scientist at Toshiba, later consultant and winner of the Deming Prize as one of Japan's post-war quality pioneers.

21 Nishibori revealed that because of his misunderstanding of English, for the first seminar, Deming used red-dyed dried 'beans' – obtained because of food rationing with some difficulty by Nishibori's housekeeper.

22 Ralph Edward Flanders (1880–1970) was another of the extraordinary characters that litter the story of OM. A mechanical engineer, industrialist, journalist and editor, banker and US Senator for Vermont. As a senator, Flanders is most famous for introducing a censure motion against Joseph McCarthy.

References

Akşin, Z., Armony, M., & Mehrotra, V. (2007). The modern call-center: A multi-disciplinary perspective on operations management research. *Production Oper. Management*, 16(6), 655–688.

Alderighi, M., Nicolini, M., & Piga, C. A. (2015). Combined effects of capacity and time on fares: Insights from the yield management of a low-cost airline. *Review of Economics and Statistics*, 97(4), 900–915.

Aldor-Noiman, S., Feigin, P. D., & Mandelbaum, A. (2009). Workload forecasting for a call center: Methodology and a case study. *Ann. Appl. Statist.*, 3(4), 1403–1447.

Armbruster, D., Gel, E. S., & Murakami, J. (2007). Bucket brigades with worker learning. *Eur. J. Oper. Res.*, 176(1), 264–274.

Armony, M., Plambeck, E., & Seshadri, S. (2009). Sensitivity of optimal capacity to customer impatience in an unobservable M/M/S queue (why you shouldn't shout at the DMV). *Manufacturing Service Oper. Management*, 11(1), 19–32.

Arrow, K. J., Harris, T., & Marshak, J. (1951). Optimal inventory policy. *Econometrica*.

Avramidis, A. N., Deslauriers, A., & L'Ecuyer, P. (2004). Modeling daily arrivals to a telephone call center. *Management Sci.*, 50, 896–908.

Bartholdi, J. J., III, & Eisenstein, D. D. (1996). A production line that balances itself. *Operations Research*, 44(1), 21–34.

Bartholdi, J. J., III, & Eisenstein, D. D. (2005). Using bucket brigades to migrate from craft manufacturing to assembly lines. *Manufacturing Service Operations Management*, 7(2), 121–129.

Bassamboo, A., & Zeevi, A. (2009). On a data-driven method for staffing large call centers. *Oper. Res.*, 57(3), 714–726.

Baybars, I. (1986). A survey of exact algorithms for the simple assembly line balancing problem. *Management Science*, 32(8), 909–932.

Bersimis, S., Psarakis, S., & Panaretos, J. (2007). Multivariate statistical process control charts: An overview. *Quality and Reliability Engineering International*, 23(5), 517–543.

Black, J. T. (2007). Design rules for implementing the Toyota Production System. *International Journal of Production Research*, 45(16), 3639–3664.

Bonabeau, E., & Meyer, C. (2001). Swarm intelligence: A whole new way to think about business. *Harvard Business Review*, 79(5), 106–115.

Boysen, N., Fliedner, M., & Scholl, A. (2007). A classification of assembly line balancing problems. *European Journal of Operational Research*, 183(2), 674–693.

Chen, R. R., Cheng, T. C. E., Choi, T. M., & Wang, Y. (2016). Novel advances in applications of the newsvendor model. *Decision Sciences*, 47, 8–10.

Cole, R. E. (1999). *Managing Quality Fads: How American Business Learned to Play the Quality Game*. Oxford: Oxford University Press.

Dantzig, G. B. (1982). Reminiscences about the origins of linear programming. *Operations Research Letters*, 1(2), April, 43–48.

Edgeworth, F. Y. (1888). The mathematical theory of banking. *Journal of the Royal Statistical Society*, 51(1), 113–127.

Erhard, M., Schoenfelder, J., Fügener, A., & Brunner, J. O. (2017). State of the art in physician scheduling. *European Journal of Operational Research*.

Erlenkotter, D. (1990). Ford Whitman Harris and the economic order quantity model. *Operations Research*, 38(6), 937–946.

Evans, J. R. (1985). An efficient implementation of the Wagner-Whitin algorithm for dynamic lot-sizing. *Journal of Operations Management*, 5(2), 229–235.

Flanders, R. E. (1925). Design, manufacture, and production control of a standard machine. *Transactions of ASME*, 26, 691–738.

Folaron, J. (2003). The evolution of Six Sigma. *Six Sigma Forum Magazine*, 2(4), 38–44.

Fujimoto, T. (1999). *The evolution of a manufacturing system at Toyota*. Oxford University Press.

Gans, N., Koole, G., & Mandelbaum, A. (2003). Telephone call centers: Tutorial, review, and research prospects. *Manufacturing & Service Operations Management*, 5(2), 79–141.

Gantt, H. L. (1903). A graphical daily balance in manufacture. *Transactions of the American Society of Mechanical Engineers*, 24, 1322–1336.

Giret, A., Trentesaux, D., & Prabhu, V. (2015). Sustainability in manufacturing operations scheduling: A state of the art review. *Journal of Manufacturing Systems*, 37, 126–140.

Hahn, G., Hill, W., Hoerl, R., & Zinkgraf, S. (1999). The impact of Six Sigma improvement: A glimpse into the future of statistics. *The American Statistician*, 53(3), 208–215.

Harris, F. W. (1913). How many parts to make at once. *Factory, The Magazine of Management*, 10(2), February, 135–136 (reprinted in Operations Research, 1990).

Heneman, H. G., & Sandver, M. G. (1977). Markov analysis in human resource administration: Applications and limitations. *Academy of Management Review*, October, 535.

Hölldobler, B., & Wilson, E. O. (2009). *The Superorganism: The Beauty, Elegance, and Strangeness of Insect Societies*. W. W. Norton & Company.

Holt, C. C., Modigliani, F., & Simon, H. A. (1955). Linear decision rule for production and employment scheduling. *Management Science*, 2, 1–30.

Holweg, M. (2007). The genealogy of lean production. *Journal of Operations Management*, 25(2), 420–437.

Hotelling, H. (1947). *Multivariable Quality Control: Illustrated by the Air Testing of Sample Bombsight*. New York: Techniques of Statistical Analysis, McGraw-Hill, pp. 110–122.

Hyer, N. L., & Wemmerlov, U. (1984). Group technology and productivity. *Harvard Business Review*, 62(4), 140–149.

Jacobs, B. W., Swink, M., & Linderman, K. (2015). Performance effects of early and late Six Sigma adoptions. *Journal of Operations Management*, 36, 244–257.

Johnson, S. M. (1954). Optimal two-and three-stage production schedules with setup times included. *Naval Research Logistics Quarterly*, 1(1), 61–68.

Kimes, S. E. (1989). Yield management: A tool for capacity-considered service firms. *Journal of Operations Management*, 8(4), 348–363.

Kopczak, L., & Lee, H. L. (2004). *Hewlett-Packard DeskJet Printer Supply Chain (A)*. Stanford Graduate School of Business.

Krafcik, J. F. (1988). Triumph of the lean production system. *Sloan Management Review*, 30(1), 41–52.

Land, H., & Doig, A. G. (1960). An automatic method of solving discrete programming problems. *Econometrica*, 28(3), 497–520.

Lapierre, S. D., & Ruiz, A. B. (2004). Balancing assembly lines: An industrial case study. *Journal of the Operational Research Society*, 55, 589–597.

Lee, H. L., & Tang, C. S. (1997). Modelling the costs and benefits of delayed product differentiation. *Management Science*, 43(1), 40–53.

Lim, Y. F., & Wu, Y. (2014). Cellular bucket brigades on U-lines with discrete work stations. *Production Oper. Management*, 23(7), 1113–1128.

Linderman, K., Schroeder, R. G., Zaheer, S., & Choo, A. S. (2003). Six Sigma: A goal-theoretic perspective. *Journal of Operations Management*, 21(2), 193–203.

Little, J. D. C., Murty, K. G., Sweeney, D. W., & Karel, C. (1963). An algorithm for the traveling salesman problem. *Operations Research*, 11(6), 972–989.

Littlewood, K. (1972), "Forecasting and Control of Passenger Bookings," AGIFORS Symposium Proceedings, 12, 95–117.

Lowry, C. A., & Montgomery, D. C. (1995). A review of multivariate control charts. *IIE Transactions*, 27, 800–810.

Lu, X. S. (1998). Control chart for multivariate attribute processes. *International Journal of Production Research*, 36(12), 3477–3489.

Marsh, E. R. (1975). The harmonogram of Karol Adamiecki. *Academy of Management Journal*, 18(2), 358–364.

McGill, J. I., & Van Ryzin, G. J. (1999). Revenue management: Research overview and prospects. *Transportation Science*, 33(2), 233–256.

Mills, E. S. (1959). Uncertainty and price theory. *Quart. J. Econom.*, 73, 116–130.

Miltenburg, J., & Wijngaard, J. (1994). The U-line line balancing problem. *Management Science*, 40, 1378–1388.

Mitrofanov, S. P. (1959). *The Scientific Principles of Group Technology* (J. L. Grayson, Trans.). Leningrad: Birmingham University.

Miyake, D. I. (2006). The shift from belt conveyor line to work-cell based assembly systems to cope with increasing demand variation in Japanese industries. *International Journal of Automotive Technology and Management*, 6(4), 419–439.

Palm, C. (1953). Methods of judging the annoyance caused by congestion. *Tele*, 4, 189–208.

Petruzzi, N. C., & Dada, M. (1999). Pricing and the newsvendor problem: A review with extensions. *Operations Research*, 47(2), 183–194.

Pinnoi, A., & Wilhelm, W. E. (1998). Assembly system design: A branch and cut approach. *Management Science*, 44, 103–118.

Pinto, P. A., Dannenbring, D. G., & Khumawala, B. M. (1983). Assembly line balancing with processing alternatives: An application. *Management Science*, 29, 817–830.

Porteus, E. L. (1985). Investing in reduced setups in the EOQ model. *Management Science*, 31(8), 998–1010.

Price, W. L., Martel, A., & Lewis, K. A. (1980). A review of mathematical models in human resource planning. *Omega*, 8(6), 639.

Ramirez, B., & Runger, G. (2006). Quantitative techniques to evaluate process stability. *Quality Engineering*, 18(1), 53–68.

Rhee, B., Schmidt, G. M., & Tsai, W. (2017). Hold safety inventory before, at, or after the fan-out point? *Production and Operations Management*, 26(5), 817–835.

Roach, B. (2005). Origin of the economic order quantity formula: Transcription or transformation? *Management Decision*, 43(9), 1262–1268.

Runger, G. C. (1996). Multivariate statistical process control for autocorrelated processes. *International Journal of Production Research*, 34(6), 1715–1724.

Salveson, M. E. (1955). The assembly line balancing problem. *The Journal of Industrial Engineering*, 6(3), 18–25.

Scholl, A., & Becker, C. (2006). State-of-the-art exact and heuristic solution procedures for simple assembly line balancing. *European Journal of Operations Research*, 168, 666–693.

Schroeder, R. G., Linderman, K., Liedtke, C., & Choo, A. S. (2008). Six Sigma: Definition and underlying theory. *Journal of Operations Management*, 26(4), 536–554.

Shah, R., & Ward, P. T. (2003). Lean manufacturing: Context, practice bundles, and performance. *Journal of Operations Management*, 21(2), 129–149.

Shah, R., & Ward, P. T. (2007). Defining and developing measures of lean production. *Journal of Operations Management*, 25(4), 785–805.

Singhal, J., & Singhal, K. (2007). Holt, Modigliani, Muth, and Simon's work and its role in the renaissance and evolution of operations management. *Journal of Operations Management*, 25(2), 300–309.

Spearman, M. L., Woodruff, D. L., & Hopp, W. J. (1990). CONWIP: A pull alternative to kanban. *The International Journal of Production Research*, 28(5), 879–894.

Spearman, M. L., & Zazanis, M. A. (1992). Push and pull production systems: Issues and comparisons. *Operations Research*, 40(3), 521–532.

Strang, D., & Kim, Y. M. (2004). The diffusion and domestication of managerial innovations: The spread of scientific management, quality circles, and TQM between the United States and Japan. In *The Oxford Handbook of Work and Organization*, Oxford University Press.

Su, J. C., Chang, Y. L., & Ferguson, M. (2005). Evaluation of postponement structures to accommodate mass customization. *Journal of Operations Management*, 23(3–4), 305–318.

Sugimori, Y., Kusunoki, K., Cho, F., & Uchikawa, S. (1977). Toyota production system and kanban system materialization of just-in-time and respect-for-human system. *The International Journal of Production Research*, 15(6), 553–564.

Swink, M., & Jacobs, B. W. (2012). Six Sigma adoption: Operating performance impacts and contextual drivers of success. *Journal of Operations Management*, 30(6), 437–453.

Tellache, N. E. H., & Boudhar, M. (2017). Two-machine flow shop problem with unit-time operations and conflict graph. *International Journal of Production Research*, 55(6), 1664–1679.

van der Rhee, B., Schmidt, G. M., & Tsai, W. (2017). Hold Safety Inventory Before, At, or After the Fan-Out Point?. *Production and Operations Management*, 26(5), 817–835.

Villa, A., & Taurino, T. (2013). From JIT to Seru, for a production as lean as possible. *Procedia Engineering*, 63, 956–965.

Wagner, H. M., & Whitin, T. M. (1958). Dynamic version of the economic lot size model. *Management Science*, 5(1), 89–96.

Webster, S., Ruben, R. A., & Yang, K. K. (2012). Impact of storage assignment decisions on a bucket brigade order picking line. *Production Operations Management*, 21(2), 276–290.

Whitin, T. M. (1955). Inventory control and price theory. *Management Science*, 2(1), 61–68.

Wilson, E. O., & Hölldobler, B. (2009). *The superorganism: The beauty, elegance, and strangeness of insect societies*. W. W Norton & Company, New York.

Womack, J. P., Womack, J. P., Jones, D. T., & Roos, D. (1990). *Machine that changed the world*. Simon and Schuster.

Womack, J. P., & Jones, D. T. (1996). Beyond Toyota: how to root out waste and pursue perfection. *Harvard Business Review*, 74(5), 140–158.

Yin, Y., Stecke, K. E., Swink, M., & Kaku, I. (2017). Lessons from seru production on manufacturing competitively in a high cost environment. *Journal of Operations Management*, 49, 67–76.

4   People

The third theme is announced by a less famous painting, *Plant and Animal Analogies* (1934–5, oil on Celotex, 61 × 76.2 cm, University of California, Irvine, Gerald Buck Collection) by Helen Lundeberg. An important US artist, she challenged the tenets of European Surrealism, the 20th-century literary, philosophical and artistic movement that explored the workings of the mind and championed the irrational. Artists like Matisse and Arp had started creating drawings using a method called automatism, whereby artists tried to allow the unconscious mind to have greater influence over the creative process. Unlike these European counterparts, Lundeberg and her US colleagues believed in employing more rational structures to depict the unconscious mind. In *Plant and Animal Analogies*, for example, black-and-white diagrams of fruit seeds and human reproductive cells float above a window ledge where a sculpted torso, a knife, a green pepper and some cherries sit. In the background a mother and child walk near a tree. The collage of images concerned with creation and life is clearly dream-like but it is not random, with dashes and arrows connecting the elements to help the viewer understand the meaning of the scene. It is this question, how to engage intellectually but truthfully with people and their thoughts and behaviours, that is the focus of this chapter. OM regularly repeats the typical exhortations that

> [s]uperior performance is ultimately based on the people in an organization. The right management principles, systems and procedures play an essential role, but the capabilities that create a competitive advantage come from people – their skill, discipline, motivation, ability to solve problems, and their capacity for learning.
>
> (Hayes et al. 1988, p. 242)

Yet, at the same time, the impact of many core OM concepts on workers in operating systems, remains under-explored. There has been 'employee-centric' OM research, not the least of which being Elton Mayo (and Roethlisberger, Dickson, etc.) and his work at the Hawthorne plant looking at the link between productivity and both environmental factors such as, infamously, the brightness of lights, humidity, etc. and psychological factors (e.g., breaks, group pressure, working hours, etc.). More recently, Powell (1995) used a resource-based model to explore the competitive impact of TQM programmes and concluded that it is "certain tacit, behavioural, imperfectly imitable features – such as open culture, employee empowerment and executive commitment – [that] can produce advantage". Lean production systems have been investigated for the role of the workplace environment (e.g., Hasle et al. 2012) and tested for potential negative employee outcomes (health and safety: Longoni et al. 2013; stress: Conti et al. 2006, etc.). Overall however, to date, OM research has placed greater emphasis on mitigating the 'problems' of workers (e.g., how to cope with the (negative) consequence of individual differences in work rates on flow-line performance: Doerr et al. 2004), than understanding the behaviours of people. Yet, as Bendoly et al. (2006) note, "[w]hen it comes to implementation, the success of operations management tools and techniques, and the accuracy of its theories, relies heavily on our understanding of human behavior" (p. 738). It is not so much that OM research has failed to recognize the importance of behavioural insights; Conway and Schultz (1959), for example, developed an impressive list of human factors that can affect operational learning performance,[1] but rather that, until recently, the field has lacked (failed to engage with) the theories and frameworks necessary to include such factors in their analyses.

People are often (at least implicitly) considered to be deterministic and predictable in their actions, act independently of others and be emotionless. Consider the earlier discussion of bucket brigades. Van Oyen et al. (2001) studied a serial production system and showed that average WIP and cycle time are minimized if all workers collaborate as a team, taking jobs successively from the queue at the front of the line and processing them through the entire line – but they also assumed that workers were identical and can readily collaborate. Given the limitations of assuming hyper-rationality, various researchers have tried to incorporate more realistic models of human behaviour. Boudreau et al. (2003) for example, raised a series of pertinent HRM challenges that need to be addressed when considering OM solutions in practice. For example, how much does worker perception of fairness affect whether and how they help each other? Similarly, there has been extensive research into operations-level effects of High-Performance Work Systems (e.g., Ichniowski and Shaw 1999) looking at team characteristics, empowerment and other practices, but explanations for the impact of these systems have been much more limited. More recently, this gap has been the focus of an increasingly significant sub-field, Behavioural OM (BeOM),[2] that has sought to apply what can be loosely called 'people-related' insights to a broad range of operations problems (Loch and Wu 2005; Gino and Pisano 2008; Bendoly et al. 2010, etc.).

What is BeOM?

Scholars agree that individual decision makers use simplifications, are influenced by others and make satisficing, not optimal choices (March and Simon 1958). Equally, organizational information processing is far from optimal, reflecting political motives and used to legitimize rather than determine courses of action, etc. (e.g., DiMaggio and Powell 1983; Feldman and March 1981). Connecting this information processing logic to OM, Dean and Bowen (1994) noted, in their comprehensive assessment of 'total' quality (TQ) that more extensive analysis of information does not necessarily lead to higher performance. Indeed, rational, comprehensive information processing might even be counterproductive under ambiguous or uncertain conditions. BeOM therefore is part of a wider effort to develop more realistic prescriptions for practice. As Bettis (2017) recently noted: "[t]he question of whether [classic MBA] theories or approaches are actually tractable for real managers working in real organizations under real-time constraints is never raised" (p. 2622). He goes on to propose a theory of "organizational intractability[3]" – basically, highlighting those circumstances when rational decision-making would take longer than a given decision remains, in its essentials, invariant. Although there has been some 'operations strategy' BeOM work – Phadnis et al. (2017) for example, studying the association between operations executives' strategic cognition and their strategic choices, with findings that seem to complement the descriptions of behavioural processes that influence top management strategic intentions (cf. Kim et al. 2014) – the majority of BeOM research to date has been concerned with quite tractable problems; studying "decisions, the behavior of individuals, or small groups of individuals" (i.e., a micro-level unit of analysis) while better recognizing that there are "non-hyper-rational actors in operational contexts" (Croson et al. 2013). Taken together these studies draw on various 'bodies of knowledge' but, to date, most commonly, cognitive psychology and social psychology (Bendoly et al. 2010).

Cognitive psychology and BeOM

Cognitive Psychology (CP) is the field of study[4] related to perceiving, attending, thinking, language and memory (American Psychological Association, Apa. org). Bendoly et al. (2010) highlight three particular areas where CP insights have "proven to be robust in a wide variety of settings, and which have immediate and important implications for OM problems". The first is overconfidence, a bias where individuals believe they know more than they do, or more specifically, believe their information is more precise than it is. The second involves estimation, anchoring decisions on otherwise irrelevant past observations and experiences (Bowman 1963) and then making insufficient adjustments to these anchored estimates in an updated context. Staats et al. (2017) for example, investigated the circumstances where cardiologists adjusted their choice between two types of stents, observing anchoring even in the presence of negative news by the Food and Drug Administration. Likewise, anchoring and adjustment have been identified as explanations for Beer Game behaviour: participants insufficiently account for orders placed but not yet received (Sterman 1989). Moritz et al. (2013) investigate anchoring and demand-chasing explanations for persistent deviations from optimal order quantities in repeated newsvendor experiments. They find that, in certain settings, individuals with higher cognitive reflection (the system 1 and system 2 notion[5] popularized by Kahneman 2011) exhibit a lower tendency to chase demand. The third area is the inter-related phenomena of loss aversion (i.e., subjective value of losing is greater than the subjective value of winning) and the reflection effect (i.e., risk attitudes depend on whether individuals are facing a gamble which involves winning or losing money: cf. Prospect Theory,[6] Kahneman and Tversky 1979). Interestingly, the broader psychological literature (e.g., Hammond and Kenneth 2000; Ariely and Zakay 2001) has also explored the ways in which individuals cope with a classic operational concern, the stress of time pressure. Time pressure may lead to worse performance in learning tasks (DeDonno and Demaree 2008) but Payne et al. (1988) suggest a hierarchy of responses. First, people try to respond by working faster but if the pressure is too high, they may begin to filter available information. If this is still insufficient, they may opt for a simpler decision-making strategy. Again, linking this concern to prospect theory, De Dreu (2003) for example, finds evidence that (perceived) time pressure, by weakening people's motivation to process information, reduces negotiation efficiency.

Social psychology and BeOM

Social Psychology (SP) bridges the gap between psychology and sociology to study how people's behaviours are the result of the interaction between mental states and social situations. Groups are a particularly significant focus for both SP and BeOM because they affect performance and productivity[7] and because, to a large extent, humans define themselves by the group memberships which form their social identity. Social loafing is strongest when a worker's individual efforts are not visible and diminishes when feedback allows people to identify individual outcomes. Schultz et al. (2003) used an experimental setting to explore social facilitation/loafing, finding support for the assertion that motivation increases for workers in groups with performance feedback. Providing the means for workers to compare their work paces motivates them to work faster. They also found no support for an "equity comparison" interpretation of social loafing (i.e., workers who assume colleagues are not working hard, reduce their own efforts in order to regain equity).

Influencing participants in an operating system via incentives/compensation is a standard managerial practice. It is the rationale behind so-called 'surge pricing' in ride-sharing platforms like Uber for example; by increasing (or decreasing) compensation at any given point in time, more (or less) drivers should be willing to participate (Cachon et al. 2017). Urda and Loch (2013) observe that in many group (operations) settings people are also strongly motivated by the relative payoffs that reflect social status, group identity and the reciprocity and fairness that characterize social relationships. They go on to highlight some potentially counter-intuitive insights that follow from this analysis. Specifically, the need to not over-emphasize "formal, extrinsic incentives" while forgetting that the "motivation of these incentives may be neutralized – or even reversed – when employees do not feel respected, treated fairly, or as members of a common group". They also argue that when managers recognize employees (status) they should also explain why any reward is deserved to maximize the emotional salience and that positive events for one member can motivate a whole team (group identity), etc. Siemsen et al. (2009) also demonstrate that (team) psychological safety is an important antecedent of group knowledge sharing, moderated by employee confidence in their knowledge. They also find – making observations that offer many connections to aspects of several 'best practice' production systems, TPS, Deming, etc. – that psychological safety increases with frequency of co-worker communication and that confidence is related to how codifiable the knowledge is.

Customers are people too?

The marketing literature has long embraced psychological insights regarding consumer behaviour. Much of this research has been applied to retail settings (a 'classic' service operation): from active management of retail environments (Machleit and Eroglu 2000) – including music (Jain and Bagdare 2011) and odours (Guéguen and Petr 2006) – to produce specific desired emotions in customers, to understanding perceptions of fairness (Goodwin and Ross 1992) and justice (Blodgett et al. 1997) when customers make complaints, etc. Equally, psychologists themselves have had a significant interest in service operations phenomena, particularly queues, as an exemplar of more general human behaviours (e.g., Osuna 1985; Ariely 1998; Ariely and Carmon 2000). Given that the involvement of the customer in the work process is a key point of difference from (buffered) manufacturing operations (Sampson and Froehle 2006), customer psychology must also be considered a critical area of BeOM research. There are numerous behavioural subjects in service OM,[8] but in this short review we will focus in on two inter-related issues: queues for service and the sequence of service elements.

Queues and queuing?

The queueing literature suggests, unsurprisingly, that queues have a recognized negative effect; being put on hold for example, leads customers to make negative inferences about the company ("too few employees, poor management, a lack of expertise on the part of the contact employee" [Unzicker 1999, p. 329]). This can mean lost customers, sales, reduced customer retention (and Customer Lifetime Value, CLV). In addition to customers 'losing' time in a queue, waiting can incur boredom and anxiety (Maister 1984; Larson 1987) that can result in unpleasant negative emotions (Hui and Tse 1996; Dabholkar and Bagozzi 2002). Furthermore, it is well known and extensively modelled (e.g., Batt and Terwiesch 2015) that excessive wait times can lead some consumers to abandon without purchase (Lu et al. 2013). Over time (!), queueing research has emphasized the important distinction between 'objective' clock time and perceived waiting time (e.g., Hui and Tse 1996; Luo et al. 2004; Yalch and Spangenberg 2000). It is perceived waiting time (i.e., consumers' own estimation of the time waited: Antonides et al. 2002) that seems to have the most influence on customer reactions (e.g., Kellaris and Mantel 1996) and, critically, consumers tend to be poor at estimating the time they are in a waiting situation. For example, Katz et al. (1991) found that bank customers overestimated their waiting time by 25% (they thought they waited 306s on average, but in fact the average was 252s). Similarly, Jones and Peppiatt (1996) observed how people waiting at a food checkout tended to overestimate perceived waiting time by 40% (221s on average) compared with objective waiting time (158s on average).

Consumers perceive occupied time as shorter, and more palatable (Zhou and Soman 2008), than unoccupied time (Jones and Peppiatt 1996; Unzicker 1999) because, when people are actively processing stimuli they perceive time as passing faster (i.e., they underestimate time). Bae and Dae-Young (2014) suggest that perceived waiting time in a restaurant can decrease when the retailer offers menu information as a method of distraction. In other words, the more information the consumer has to process while waiting, such as making choices with a large number of options, the more difficult it will be to calculate the waiting time, which results in underestimations of time (Fasolo et al. 2009). Providing entertainments such as bands, jugglers and clowns can reduce perceived waiting time (Dickson et al. 2005), but research shows that something as passive as music being played can distract attention from the passage of time (Oakes 2003; Mukherjee et al. 2009). Consequently, insight is that perceived waiting time can be affected by managerial/service design actions (Antonides et al. 2002).

Queues do not always have negative consequences[9] for an operation (Raz and Ert 2008; Veeraraghavan and Debo 2009; Giebelhausen et al. 2011; Debo et al. 2012). In certain cases, they can signal quality (with consumers asking themselves, if the quality of this product/service is low, why would there be a long line?) and actually attract more customers (Giebelhausen et al. 2011; Kremer and Debo 2015). Related work finds that consumers can infer products are more valuable when others are waiting behind them in a line (Koo and Fishbach 2011). In such circumstance, service providers might consider slowing down service rate to signal high quality via long lines (the old queue outside a nightclub trick) – even if some customers might abandon (Debo et al. 2012). It is also possible that a long wait could increase consumption for other, less than rational reasons. Even if frustrated, some consumers in a long queue might eventually make a larger purchase, to try to 'recoup' the sunk-cost of waiting (Thaler 1985; Arkes and Blumer 1985). The sunk-cost fallacy is another 'classic' CP bias that addresses people's tendency to persist in a course of action that they would otherwise not pursue, given some earlier investment (Navarro and Fantino 2009). Mandelbaum and Zeltyn (2013) for example, found that call-centre customers who had waited for a significant time tended to remain patient.

That said, the simple application of a sunk-cost logic to waiting is a subject of ongoing debate, specifically the extent to which very different types of costs (i.e., financial and temporal) are interchangeable. In other words, just how true is the classic assertion that "time is money"? Time has a certain value due to its scarcity (Jacoby et al. 1976), but to what extent can temporal (opportunity) costs (Becker 1965; Soman 2001) really be calculated in monetary terms (i.e., is an hour spent in a queue equivalent to an hour's worth of wages?). Lin et al. (2015) for example, applied prospect theory in a time gain-and-loss context and their combined results suggest that participants held different perceptions of the value of "short time" versus "little money". In other words, they preferred saving an extra 2 minutes on one occasion to saving 1 minute on two occasions and preferred waiting an extra 1 minute two times to waiting an extra 2 minutes one time. Some research suggests that the way time is valued depends on the context. Kumar and Krishnamurthy (2008) for example, suggest that congestion aversion is more dominant than risk aversion regarding wait times (i.e., customers will risk a longer wait to avoid congestion). Now consider the implications of these behavioural insights in the case of overbooking, a common practice for airline companies, hotels, etc. to minimize losses from cancellations and no-shows (Kimes and Chase 1998). On those occasions when all the passengers who have booked show up, airlines ask for volunteers who will give up their seats, typically for a certain amount of compensation. If time has a specific monetary value, should those passengers who booked earlier expect a higher level of compensation (Park and Jang 2014)? Consequently, in addition to monetary and availability concerns, travellers' behavioural intentions are very much to the fore.

Sequence and sequencing

Since Maister (1985, p. 117) noted that, when a service experience takes place over an extended period of time, customers perceive pre-process waiting (i.e., the part of the service encounter *before* the official service delivery begins) differently from in-process waiting, it has become increasingly clear that satisfaction is not just about (even perceived) service duration(s) but also the relationship in time of the various service elements (Hsee and Abelson 1991). Bolton et al. (2006) found that the sequence of service experiences – as measured by average engineer work-minutes per contract – can predict renewal rates of support service contracts. Soman and Shi (2003) found that "in choosing between two services that cover the same displacement in the same time, consumer choice is driven by the perception of progress toward the goal" (p. 1129) such that satisfaction with a waiting experience increases or decreases over time depending on the customers' perceptions of how much closer they are to their goal. Noting that this would only apply in service settings that are goal oriented rather than process oriented, Bitran et al. (2008) argue that this could provide an explanation for Maister's *pre-* versus *in-process* observations. Of course, customer satisfaction still depends on what happens but service elements are often transient and experienced fleetingly, meaning that both *when something happens* and *how it is remembered* are critical, challenging largely static and discrete conceptualization of both expectations and disconfirmation in much of the satisfaction literature (e.g., Carmon and Kahneman 1996). When remembering the 'overall experience' customers can focus on a range of features[10] including, but not limited to, duration/queues (Ariely 1998; Ariely and Zauberman 2000; Ariely and Carmon 2000; Ariely and Zakay 2001). In other words, despite its core position in OM research, duration may not be salient in many service settings. Moreover, given the tendency to overlook individuals in such research, it is important to note that the attention anyone pays to the passage of time also depends on personality traits such as public self-consciousness. If someone exhibits a high degree of awareness of the self as it is viewed by others this can result in self-monitoring and social anxiety, and it is likely they will fix more on the duration of a public queue (Marquis and Filiatrault 2003). In short, making general statements about the problem of waiting is a challenge. Duration clearly matters most in those situations where it is the main attribute (e.g., choosing a supermarket line or travelling or buying 'fast' food), and because of commodification is a measurable dimension of performance, but beyond that queues may matter much less than expected[11]?

Psychological and Service OM research shows that combining both static (e.g., the peak intensity and intensity at the end of an experience) and dynamic intensity characteristics (e.g., positioning of events over time, the trend and rate of change) allows for a fuller evaluation of service sequences (e.g., Chase and Dasu 2001; Ariely and Zauberman 2000; Bitran et al. 2008; Dixon and Verma 2013). Heskett et al. (1990) for example, introduced the idea of the "service bookend", also stressing the need for services to provide a strong beginning. Similarly, Johnston (1995) proposed that exceeding a customer's expectation early in an encounter is more likely to delight the customer throughout the service encounter because the customer is primed to see good service. There are significant managerial implications of service sequence, with some research finding a preference for improving sequence intensity profiles such that peak intensity[12] at the end of an experience, creates an upward trend. In an interesting extension of this sequencing work, Dixon et al. (2017) explored, using scenario experiments, how the overall perception of a service experience is impacted when the peak is a surprise. In addition to confirming the positive influence of ending with a strong peak, they found that the remembered experience of a surprise peak (wherever it was in the service sequence) positively affects customer perceptions and that a surprise peak ending has a lasting effect that amplifies the peak-end effect of remembered experiences.

A final theme related to the question of service design and sequence is that of "whether the experience is perceived to be composed of single or multiple parts" (Ariely and Zauberman 2000, p. 219). Noting that, in general, "improving sequences are preferable to deteriorating ones", Ariely and Zauberman (2000) make specific recommendations for what they label the 'partitioning' of services. Services that are generally improving should not be partitioned. Services that are declining should be partitioned. Then more specifically, "partitioning at [a peak] is preferable and should lead to higher evaluations" and "when externally imposed partitioning occurs, effort to provide more satisfying experiences for customers would be better placed before rather than after this partitioning" (p. 138). Bitran et al. (2008) suggest this idea of, what they call, 'service cohesiveness' offer (another) explanation of why pre-process waits are "more annoying than in-process waits". In-process waits are,

> by definition, integrated into a service encounter that, if resolved positively, will contain a strong positive end effect. The pre-process wait, on the other

hand, ends just before service begins, so the end effect is at a low point of the customer experience.

(Bitran et al. 2008)

They go on to note that the broader operational (and marketing/communications) challenge is "to be able to integrate the entire service encounter in situations with positive ends and to segregate the segments when the global ending (the end of the last segment) is negative".

Concluding comments

For all the promise and potential of BeOM, it is important to note two related concerns. First, psychology is suffering something of a crisis. Although such worries are not new – Freud's theories were labelled pseudoscience by Karl Popper because they could not be falsified – it is clear that, at a time when psychology has never had such reach (into adjacent fields such as Economics (Camerer 1999), in the popular consciousness, etc.), scholars have struggled to replicate many of its most intriguing findings. Most (in)famously, the Bargh et al. (1996) study of 'priming' (exposure to one stimulus sub-consciously influences responses to subsequent stimulus) affecting action which has been to date cited more than 4500 times[13] concluded that reading words related to elderliness (e.g., "Florida", "Bingo") caused subjects to walk more slowly. This 'replication crisis' (e.g., Maxwell et al. 2015) has led to a great deal of soul-searching in psychology and significant attempts to both undertake and publish more replication studies and also address questionable research practices (QRPs); such as collecting data until a significant result was obtained and excluding data after analysis. Second, any interdisciplinary endeavour brings risks; that core assumptions will be missed, key findings misinterpreted and that only partial perspectives are imported. Specifically, Katsikopoulos and Gigerenzer (2013) warn that, to date, BeOM may have over-emphasized one perspective on the managerial use of heuristics (those simple 'rules of thumb' that lead to rapid decision-making with limited information and computation: cf. March 1994), viewing them as a liability/limitation. This emphasis arguably reflects the broader impact of the bias and heuristic work of Tversky, Kahneman and colleagues (Kahneman et al. 1982). Although they themselves present a balanced perspective ("heuristics are quite useful, but sometimes they lead to severe and systematic errors": Tversky and Kahneman 1974, p. 1124) the dissemination of this research has led to 'widely published claims that human judgment abilities are poor' (Lopes 1991, p. 65). For example, some of the foundational articles in BeOM (and BeSCM), such as Croson and Donohue (2006), Carter et al. (2007) and Gino and Pisano (2008) focus on cognitive limitations. Similarly, Su (2008) built a behavioural newsvendor model by combining a utility function with the quantal response framework (a solution concept in game theory) but, although this approach incorporates bounded rationality, the logic is that players tend to make errors when choosing which strategy.

There is mounting evidence, however, that less deliberative forms of cognition are actually central to skilled functioning. Katsikopoulos and Gigerenzer (2013, p. 5) for example, argue persuasively, for a richer perspective that includes the more positive notion of 'fast-and-frugal-heuristics' (Gigerenzer and Gaissmaier 2011; Bertel and Kirlik 2010; Gigerenzer and Goldstein 1996). The efficacy of these heuristics has been discussed in behavioural strategy (Bingham and Eisenhardt 2011; Levinthal 2011) and marketing (Wuebben and von Wagenheim 2008[14]) but not, as yet, BeOM. As an illustration, consider the take-the-best heuristic. This is used when making a decision based on inferences about a situation. According to Gigerenzer and Goldstein (1996) people use experience to sort various criteria into order and then, rather than considering all of the reasons, make inferences based on the 'most important' reason. Then, if the most important reason is invalidated, a decision-maker will tend to work her way down through the ordered list. Perhaps what is most interesting about this body of work is that scholars have also identified the general conditions under which fast and frugal heuristics perform well or less well (Katsikopoulos 2011). For example, models of heuristics tend to perform better than more mathematically sophisticated models when the sample available to calibrate parameters is small. Ultimately, such concerns should not lead us to conclude that either all psychological findings are unreliable or BeOM work to date is fatally limited. In many ways these observations indicate just how much scope there is for novel work in the BeOM sub-field but they should also remind us to be careful (as part of a more general precautionary principle perhaps?) when we incorporate adjacent theoretical constructs. This is a theme we return to in the final chapter.

One final comment on attempts to better include 'people' in OM is to note the limited role that considerations of gender have played in research to date. As part of the BeOM dialogue, De Vericourt et al. (2013) experimented with the role that gender differences played in different ordering behaviour and risk taking in the newsvendor problem[15] and the recent Metters (2017) study concludes that gender effects shape extreme international differences in the viability of certain operational practices. This question of global operations and female workers is particularly interesting as, for the last 25 years, women – especially in the global south – have increasingly staffed the firms serving transnational business. Such operating arrangements have been the subject of extensive OM study but there is much less insight regarding the men *and* women who work in these factories, call centres, software houses, law firms, etc. As a stark example, the garment trade in Bangladesh has grown rapidly over the past 25 years, and today accounts for 80% of total exports. There are now 4,825 garment factories in Bangladesh employing over three million people and 85% of these workers are women. This limitation contrasts strongly with numerous discussions of the role of national culture in OM (e.g., Metters et al. 2010). Intriguingly, Hofstede's (2001) framework for characterizing national cultures has been widely used (e.g., Gray and Massimino 2014) as a parsimonious and testable framework for such analyses and this offers five dimensions: uncertainty avoidance, long-term orientation, power-distance, individualism and masculinity. It can only be concluded that gender represents a significant gap and considerable opportunity for future scholarship.

Notes

1 As noted by Adler and Clark (1991), various OM works have described individual and group factors that affect operational learning: Hirschmann (1964), Hollander (1965), Baloff (1970), Hayes and Wheelwright (1984), etc.

2 There is now the POMS College of Behavior in Operations Management, the INFORMS Behavioral Operations Management Section, various special issues in top-tier journals, etc.

3 He positions his idea as analogous to the notion of computational intractability; the observation that computation still takes time and memory. Bettis cites Yanofsky who noted (albeit in 2013) that the classic OM "traveling salesman", parameterized for 100 cities, will, with a computer that can check a million routes a second, take roughly 2.9 × 10142 centuries to find the global shortest route.

4 WWII also features heavily in the Cognitive Psychology story. In seeking to train soldiers to use new technology, find ways to maintain focus under duress, etc. the work of Donald Broadbent and others paved the way for what would become cognitive psychology.

5 System 1 processes are typically described as intuitive, tacit, contextualized and rapid while System 2 processes are reflective, analytical and rely on abstract reasoning.

6 Another, very popular, CP theory proposed by Kahneman and Tversky that describes (rather than prescribes) the way people choose between probabilistic alternatives that involve risk. It suggests that people make decisions based on the potential value of losses and gains rather than the final outcome, and that people evaluate these losses and gains using heuristics.

7 Social facilitation is the tendency to work harder and faster in the presence of others whereas social loafing is the tendency of individuals to slack off when working in a group.

8 The boundary between service operations and marketing is always more porous and hence wait time, etc. has also featured heavily in marketing research. Pyone and Isen (2011) show that consumers in a positive affect condition are more willing to wait because they do not focus their attention on the wait itself but on their emotions. Research suggests that longer waits increase boredom, highlighting levels of anxiety and stress (e.g., Miller et al. 2007).

9 In some cultures, elders like to socialize when standing in queues, and they therefore prefer longer waits (Rafaeli et al. 2002).

10 The so-called gestalt components of the experience are those on which customers focus when making their overall evaluations. Ariely and Carmon (2000) highlight three key sets of features: (1) the rate at which the service encounter becomes more or less positive/negative over time, and the overall trend of the experience; (2) the intensity of pleasure or discomfort experienced at peaks and troughs; and (3) the intensity of pleasure or discomfort experienced at the end of the service encounter.

11 For instance, if you ask a friend about their recent vacation, do you expect/want the answer to focus on its duration? (Ariely and Zakay 2001, p. 201).

12 Ariely and Carmon (2000) found that weight assigned to peaks (and troughs) decreases as customers become more familiar with an experience.

13 It should be noted that some of the explanation comes from a systemic bias – not exclusive to psychology – whereby editors and reviewers can emphasize the publication of intriguing or unusual findings. They may never be replicated but they attract lots of attention/impact. Equally, the process of replicating others work is deemed unattractive and typically relegated to less prestigious journals.

14 They discuss the reliance of experienced airline and apparel managers on the hiatus heuristic: 'Classify a customer as active when the number of months since a customer's last purchase, t, is less than 9'. Unfortunately for academics, who have been investigating this type of question for more than 30 years using various sophisticated

predictive techniques, Wuebben and von Wagenheim (2008) found the hiatus heuristic, with its single attribute and ignorance of full purchase history, resulted in more accurate predictions.

15 Interestingly, this paper has been widely cited but not in follow-on gender-related research.

References

Adler, P. S., & Clark, K. B. (1991). Behind the learning curve: A sketch of the learning process. *Management Science*, 37(3), 267–281.

Antonides, G., Verhoef, P. C., & Van Aalst, M. (2002). Consumer perception and evaluation of waiting time: A field experiment. *Journal of Consumer Psychology*, 12(3), 193–202.

Ariely, D. (1998). Combining experiences over time: The effects of duration, intensity changes and on-line measurements on retrospective pain evaluations. *J. Behav. Decision Making*, 11, 19–45.

Ariely, D., & Carmon, Z. (2000). Gestalt characteristics of experiences: The defining features of summarized events. *J. Behav. Decision Making*, 13(2), 191–201.

Ariely, D., & Loewenstein, G. (2000). When does duration matter in judgment and decision making? *J. Experiment. Psych. General*, 129(4), 508–523.

Ariely, D., & Zakay, D. (2001). A timely account of the role of duration in decision making. *Acta Psychologica*, 108(2), 187–207.

Ariely, D., & Zauberman, G. (2000). On the making of an experience: The effects of breaking and combining experiences on their overall evaluation. *J. Behav. Decision Making*, 13, 219–232.

Arkes, H. R., & Blumer, C. (1985). The psychology of sunk cost. *Organizational Behavior and Human Decision Processes*, 35(1), 124–140.

Bae, G., & Kim, D. Y. (2014). The effects of offering menu information on perceived waiting time. *Journal of Hospitality Marketing & Management*, 23(7), 746–767.

Baloff, N. (1970). Startup management. *IEEE Transactions on Engineering Management*, (4), 132–141.

Bargh, J. A., Chen, M., & Burrows, L. (1996). Automaticity of social behavior: Direct effects of trait construct and stereotype activation on action. *Journal of Personality and Social Psychology*, 71(2), 230.

Batt, R. J., & Terwiesch, C. (2015). Waiting patiently: An empirical study of queue abandonment in an emergency department. *Management Science*, 61(1), 39–59.

Becker, G. S. (1965). A Theory of the Allocation of Time. *The Economic Journal*, 493–517.

Bendoly, E. (2016). Fit, bias, and enacted sensemaking in data visualization: Frameworks for continuous development in operations and supply chain management analytics. *Journal of Business Logistics*, 37(1), 6–17.

Bendoly, E., Croson, R., Goncalves, P., & Schultz, K. (2010). Bodies of knowledge for research in behavioral operations. *Production and Operations Management*, 19(4), 434–452.

Bendoly, E., Donohue, K., & Schultz, K. L. (2006). Behavior in operations management: Assessing recent findings and revisiting old assumptions. *Journal of Operations Management*, 24(6), 737–752.

Bernstein, E. S. (2012). The transparency paradox: A role for privacy in organizational learning and operational control. *Administrative Science Quarterly*, 57(2), 181–216.

Bertel, S., & Kirlik, A. (2010). Fast and frugal heuristics. In *Wiley Encyclopedia of Operations Research and Management Science*, John Wiley and Sons Ltd.

Bettis, R. A. (2017). Organizationally intractable decision problems and the intellectual virtues of heuristics. *Journal of Management*, 43(8), 2620–2637.

Bingham, C. B., & Eisenhardt, K. M. (2011). Rational heuristics: the 'simple rules' that strategists learn from process experience. *Strategic Management Journal*, 32(13), 1437–1464.

Bitran, G. R., Ferrer, J. C., & Rocha e Oliveira, P. (2008). OM forum: Managing customer experiences: Perspectives on the temporal aspects of service encounters. *Manufacturing & Service Operations Management*, 10(1), 61–83.

Blodgett, J. G., Hill, D. J., & Tax, S. S. (1997). The effects of distributive, procedural, and interactional justice on postcomplaint behavior. *Journal of Retailing*, 73(2), 185–210.

Bolton, R. N., Lemon, K. N., & Bramlett, M. D. (2006). The effect of service experiences over time on a supplier's retention of business customers. *Management Science*, 52(12), 1811–1823.

Boudreau, J., Hopp, W., McClain, J. O., & Thomas, L. J. (2003). On the interface between operations and human resources management. *Manufacturing & Service Operations Management*, 5(3), 179–202.

Bowen, D. E., & Schneider, B. (1985). Boundary spanning role employees and the service encounter: Some guidelines for management research. In J. A. Czepiel, M. R. Soloman, & C. F. Surprenant (eds), *The Service Encounter*. Lexington, MA: Lexington Books.

Bowman, E. H. (1963). Consistency and optimality in managerial decision making. *Management Science*, 9(2), 310–321.

Brown, K. A. (2000). Predicting safe employee behaviour in the steel industry: The development and test of a socio-technical model. *Journal of Operations Management*, 18(4), 445–468.

Cachon, G. P., Daniels, K. M., & Lobel, R. (2017). The role of surge pricing on a service platform with self-scheduling capacity. *Manufacturing & Service Operations Management*, 19(3), 368–384.

Carmon, Z., & Kahneman, D. (1996). *The experienced utility of queuing: real time affect and retrospective evaluations of simulated queues*. Duke University: Durham, NC, USA.

Carter, C. R., Kaufmann, L., & Michel, A. (2007). Behavioral supply management: A taxonomy of judgment and decision-making biases. *International Journal of Physical Distribution and Logistics Management*, 37(8), 631–669.

Camerer, C. (1999). Behavioral economics: Reunifying psychology and economics. *Proceedings of the National Academy of Sciences of the United States of America*, 96, 10575–10577.

Chase, R. B., & Dasu, S. (2001). Want to perfect your company's service? Use behavioral science. *Harvard Business Review*, 79(6), 78–84.

Choi, S., & Mattila, A. S. (2008). Perceived controllability and service expectation: Influences on customer reactions following service failure. *Journal of Business Research*, 61(1), 24–30.

Conti, R., Angelis, J., Cooper, C., Faragher, B., & Gill, C. (2006). The effects of lean production on worker job stress. *International Journal of Operations and Production Management*, 26(9), 1013–1038.

Conway, R. W., & Schultz, A. (1959). The manufacturing progress function. *Journal of Industrial Engineering*, 10(1), 39–54.

Croson, R., & Donohue, K. (2006). Behavioral causes of the bullwhip effect and the observed value of inventory information. *Management Science*, 52(3), 323–336.

Croson, R., Schultz, K., Siemsen, E., & Yeo, M. L. (2013). Behavioral operations: The state of the field. *Journal of Operations Management*, 31(1–2), 1–5.

Dabholkar, P. A., & Bagozzi, R. P. (2002). An attitudinal model of technology-based self-service: moderating effects of consumer traits and situational factors. *Journal of the Academy of Marketing Science*, 30(3), 184–201.

Dean Jr, J. W., & Bowen, D. E. (1994). Management theory and total quality: Improving research and practice through theory development. *Academy of Management Review*, 19(3), 392–418.

Debo, L. G., Parlour, C., & Rajan, U. (2012). Signaling quality via queues. *Management Science*, 58(5), 876–891.

DeDonno, M. A., & Demaree, H. A. (2008). Perceived time pressure and the Iowa Gambling Task. *Judgment and Decision Making*, 3(8), 636.

De Dreu, C. K. (2003). Time pressure and closing of the mind in negotiation. *Organizational Behavior and Human Decision Processes*, 91(2), 280–295.

De Vericourt, F., Jain, K., Bearden, J. N., & Filipowicz, A. (2013). Sex, risk and the newsvendor. *Journal of Operations Management*, 31(1–2), 86–92.

Dickson, D., Ford, R. C., & Laval, B. (2005). Managing real and virtual waits in hospitality and service organizations. *Cornell Hotel and Restaurant Administration Quarterly*, 46(1), 52–68.

Dixon, M. J., & Verma, R. (2013). Sequence effects in service bundles: Implications for service design and scheduling. *Journal of Operations Management*, 31(3), 138–152.

Dixon, M. J., Victorino, L., Kwortnik, R. J., & Verma, R. (2017). Surprise, anticipation, and sequence effects in the design of experiential services. *Production and Operations Management*, 26(5), 945–960.

Doerr, K. H., Freed, T., Mitchell, T. R., Schriesheim, C. A., & Zhou, X. T. (2004). Work flow policy and within-worker and between-workers variability in performance. *Journal of Applied Psychology*, 89(5), 911.

Doerr, K. H., & Gue, K. R. (2013). A performance metric and goal-setting procedure for deadline-oriented processes. *Production and Operations Management*, 22(3), 726–738.

Ellway, B. (2016). Design vs practice: How problematic call routing and rerouting restructures the call centre service system. *International Journal of Operations & Production Management*, 36(4), 408–428.

Fasolo, B., Carmeci, F. A., & Misuraca, R. (2009). The effect of choice complexity on perception of time spent choosing: When choice takes longer but feels shorter. *Psychology & Marketing*, 26(3), 213–228.

Feldman, M. S., & March, J. G. (1981). Information in organizations as signal and symbol. *Administrative Science Quarterly*, 171–186.

Giebelhausen, M. D., Robinson, S. G., & Cronin Jr, J. J. (2011). Worth waiting for: Increasing satisfaction by making consumers wait. *Journal of the Academy of Marketing Science*, 39(6), 889–905.

Gigerenzer, G., & Goldstein, D. G. (1996). Reasoning the fast and frugal way: Models of bounded rationality. *Psychol. Rev.*, 103, 650–669.

Gigerenzer, G., & Gaissmaier, W. (2011). Heuristic decision making. *Annu. Rev. Psychol.*, 62, 451–482.

Gino, F., & Pisano, G. (2008). Toward a theory of behavioral operations. *Manufacturing & Service Operations Management*, 10(4), 676–691.

Goodwin, C., & Ross, I. (1992). Consumer responses to service failures: Influence of procedural and interactional fairness perceptions. *Journal of Business Research*, 25(2), 149–163.

Gray, J. V., & Massimino, B. (2014). The effect of language differences and national culture on operational process compliance. *Production and Operations Management*, 23(6), 1042–1056.

Guéguen, N., & Petr, C. (2006). Odors and consumer behavior in a restaurant. *International Journal of Hospitality Management*, 25(2), 335–339.

Hammond, K. R., & Kenneth, R. (2000). *Judgments under stress*. Oxford University Press on Demand.

Hasle, P., Bojesen, A., Langaa, J. P., & Bramming, P. (2012). Lean and the working environment: A review of the literature. *International Journal of Operations & Production Management*, 32(7), 829–849.

Hayes, R. H., & Wheelwright, S. C. (1984). *Restoring our competitive edge: competing through manufacturing*, Wiley, NY.

Hayes, R. H., Wheelwright, S. C., & Clark, K. B. (1988). *Dynamic manufacturing: Creating the learning organization*. Simon and Schuster.

Hart, C. W., Heskett, J. L., & Sasser, J. W. (1990). The profitable art of service recovery. *Harvard Business Review*, 68(4), 148–156.

Hofstede, G. (2001). *Culture's Consequences*. 2nd ed. Thousand Oaks, CA: Sage.

Hollander, S. (1965). *The sources of increased efficiency: A study of DuPont rayon plants*. MIT Press Books.

Hopp, W. J., Iravani, S. M. R., Yuen, G. R. (2007). Operations systems with discretionary task completion. *Management Science*, 53(1), 61–77.

Hirschmann, W. B. (1964). Profit from the learning-curve. *Harvard Business Review*, 42(1), 125–139.

Hsee, C. K., & Abelson, R. P. (1991). Velocity relation: Satisfaction as a function of the first derivative of outcome over time. *Journal of personality and social psychology*, 60(3), 341.

Hui, M. K., & Tse, D. K. (1996). What to tell consumers in waits of different lengths: An integrative model of service evaluation. *Journal of Marketing*, 60(2), 81–90.

Ichniowski, C., & Shaw, K. (1999). The effects of human resource management systems on economic performance: An international comparison of US and Japanese plants. *Management Science*, 45(5), 704–721.

Jacoby, J., Szybillo, G. J., & Berning, C. K. (1976). Time and consumer behavior: An interdisciplinary overview. *Journal of Consumer Research*, 2(4), 320–339.

Jain, R., & Bagdare, S. (2011). Music and consumption experience: A review. *International Journal of Retail & Distribution Management*, 39(4), 289–302.

Johnston, R. (1995). The determinants of service quality: satisfiers and dissatisfiers. *International Journal of Service Industry Management*, 6(5), 53–71.

Jones, P., & Peppiatt, E. (1996). Managing perceptions of waiting times in service queues. *International Journal of Service Industry Management*, 7(5), 47–61.

Kahneman, D. (2011). *Thinking, Fast and Slow*. New York: Farrar, Straus and Giroux.

Kahneman, D. & Tversky A.(1979). Prospect theory: an analysis of decision under risk, *Econometrica*, 47(2), 363–391.

Kahneman, D., Slovic, P., & Tversky, A. (1982). *Judgment Under Uncertainty: Heuristics and Biases*. Cambridge, UK: Cambridge University Press.

Katsikopoulos, K. V. (2011). Psychological heuristics for making inferences: Definition, performance, and the emerging theory and practice. *Decision Analysis*, 8(1), 10–29.

Katsikopoulos, K. V., & Gigerenzer, G. (2013). Behavioral operations management: A blind spot and a research program. *Journal of Supply Chain Management*, 49(1), 3–7.

Katz, K.L., Larson, B.M., & Larson, R.C. (1991). Prescription for the waiting-in-line blues: Entertain, enlighten, and engage. *Sloan Management Review*, (Winter), 44–53.

Kaufmann, L., Michel, A., & Carter, C. R. (2009). Debiasing strategies in supply management decision making. *Journal of Business Logistics*, 30(1), 85–106.

Kellaris, J. J., & Mantel, S. P. (1996). Shaping time perceptions with background music: The effect of congruity and arousal on estimates of ad durations. *Psychology & Marketing*, 13(5), 501–515.

Kelman, M. G. (2011). *The Heuristics Debate*. New York, NY: Oxford University Press.

Kim, Y. H., Sting, F. J., & Loch, C. H. (2014). Top-down, bottom-up, or both? Toward an integrative perspective on operations strategy formation. *Journal of Operations Management*, 32(7–8), 462–474.

Koo, M., & Fishbach, A. (2010). A silver lining of standing in line: Queuing increases value of products. *Journal of Marketing Research*, 47(4), 713–724.

Kimes, S. E., & Chase, R. B. (1998). The strategic levers of yield management. *Journal of Service Research*, 1(2), 156–166.

Kremer, M., & Debo, L. (2015). Inferring quality from wait time. *Management Science*, 62(10), 3023–3038.

Kumar, P., & Krishnamurthy, P. (2008). The impact of service-time uncertainty and anticipated congestion on customers' waiting-time decisions. *Journal of Service Research*, 10(3), 282–292.

Larson, R. C. (1987). OR forum: Perspectives on queues: Social justice and the psychology of queueing. *Operations Research*, 35(6), 895–905.

Leclerc, F., Schmitt, B. H., & Dube, L. (1995). Waiting time and decision making: Is time like money? *Journal of Consumer Research*, 22(1), 110–119.

Levinthal, D. A. (2011). A behavioral approach to strategy: What's the alternative? *Strategic Management Journal*, 32(13), 1517–1523.

Li, Xin, Guo, P., & Lian, Z. (2016). Quality-speed competition in customer-intensive services with boundedly rational customers. *Production and Operations Management*, 25(11), 1885–1901.

Liang, C.-C. (2016). Queueing management and improving customer experience: Empirical evidence regarding enjoyable queues. *Journal of Consumer Marketing*, 33(4), 257–268.

Lin, Y. T., Xia, K. N., & Bei, L. T. (2015). Customer's perceived value of waiting time for service events. *Journal of Consumer Behaviour*, 14(1), 28–40.

Linderman, K., Schroeder, R. G., & Choo, A. S. (2006). Six Sigma: The role of goals in improvement teams. *Journal of Operations Management*, 24(6), 779–790.

Liu, N., Finkelstein, S. R., Kruk, M. E., & Rosenthal, D. (2017). When waiting to see a doctor is less irritating: Understanding patient preferences and choice behavior in appointment scheduling. *Management Science*, 64(5), 1975–1996.

Loch, C., & Wu, Y. (2005). Behavioral operations management. *Foundations and Trends in Technology, Information, and Operations Management*, 1(3), 121–232.

Loch, C., & Wu, Y. (2008). Social preferences and supply chain performance: An experimental study. *Management Science*, 54(11), 1835–1849.

Longoni, A., Pagell, M., Johnston, D., & Veltri, A. (2013). When does lean hurt?: An exploration of lean practices and worker health and safety outcomes. *International Journal of Production Research*, 51(11), 3300–3320.

Lopes, L. L. (1991). The rhetoric of irrationality. *Theory and Psychology*, 1(1), 65–82.

Lu, Y., Musalem, A., Olivares, M., & Schilkrut, A. (2013). Measuring the effect of queues on customer purchases. *Management Science*, 59(8), 1743–1763.

Luo, W., Liberatore, M. J., Nydick, R. L., Chung, Q. B., & Sloane, E. (2004). Impact of process change on customer perception of waiting time: a field study. *Omega*, 32(1), 77–83.

Machleit, K. A., & Eroglu, S. A. (2000). Describing and measuring emotional response to shopping experience. *Journal of Business Research*, 49(2), 101–111.

Maister, D. H. (1984). *The Psychology of Waiting Lines*. Boston, MA: Harvard Business School.

Maister, D. H. (1985). The psychology of waiting lines. In J. Czepiel, M. Solomon, C. Suprenant (eds.), *The Service Encounter: Managing Employee/Customer Interaction in Service Businesses* (pp. 113–123). Lexington, MA: Lexington Books.

Mantel, S. P., Tatikonda, M. V., & Liao, Y. (2006). A behavioral study of supply manager decision-making: Factors influencing make versus buy evaluation. *Journal of Operations Management*, 24(6), 822–838.

Mandelbaum, A., & Zeltyn, S. (2013). Data-stories about (im) patient customers in tele-queues. *Queueing Systems*, 75(2–4), 115–146.

Marquis, M., & Filiatrault, P. (2003). Public self-consciousness disposition effect on reactions to waiting in line. *J. Consumer Behav.*, 2(3), 212–232.

Maxwell, S. E., Lau, M. Y., & Howard, G. S. (2015). Is psychology suffering from a replication crisis? What does "failure to replicate" really mean? *American Psychologist*, 70(6), 487.

Metters, R. (2017). Gender and operations management. *Cross Cultural & Strategic Management*, 24(2), 350–364.

Metters, R., Zhao, X., Bendoly, E., Jiang, B., & Young, S. (2010). The way that can be told of is not an unvarying way: Cultural impacts on Operations Management in Asia. *Journal of Operations Management*, 28(3), 177–185.

Miller, E. G., Kahn, B. E., & Luce, M. F. (2007). Consumer wait management strategies for negative service events: a coping approach. *Journal of Consumer Research*, 34(5), 635–648.

Moritz, B. B., Hill, A. V., & Donohue, K. L. (2013). Individual differences in the newsvendor problem: Behavior and cognitive reflection. *Journal of Operations Management*, 31(1–2), 72–85.

Mukherjee, A., Malhotra, N., Whiting, A., & Donthu, N. (2009). Closing the gap between perceived and actual waiting times in a call center: results from a field study. *Journal of Services Marketing*.

Navarro, A. D., & Fantino, E. (2009). The sunk-time effect: An exploration. *Journal of Behavioral Decision Making*, 22(3), 252–270.

Oakes, S. (2003). Musical tempo and waiting perceptions. *Psychology & Marketing*, 20(8), 685–705.

Osuna, E. E. (1985). The psychological cost of waiting. *Journal of Mathematical Psychology*, 29(1), 82–105.

Park, J. Y., & Jang, S. S. (2014). Sunk costs and travel cancellation: Focusing on temporal cost. *Tourism Management*, 40, 425–435.

Payne, J. W., Bettman, J. R., & Johnson, E. J. (1988). Adaptive strategy selection in decision making. *Journal of Experimental Psychology: Learning, Memory, and Cognition*, 14(3), 534.

Phadnis, S. S., Sheffi, Y., Caplice, C., & Singh, M. (2017). Strategic cognition of operations executives. *Production and Operations Management*, 26(12), 2323–2337.

Powell, T. C. (1995). Total quality management as competitive advantage: A review and empirical study. *Strategic Management Journal*, 16(1), 15–37.

Pulles, N. J., & Hartman, P. (2017). Likeability and its effect on outcomes of interpersonal interaction. *Industrial Marketing Management*, 66, 56–63.

Pyone, J. S., & Isen, A. M. (2011). Positive affect, intertemporal choice, and levels of thinking: Increasing consumers' willingness to wait. *Journal of Marketing Research*, 48(3), 532–543.

Raab, M., & Gigerenzer, G. (2015). The power of simplicity: A fast-and-frugal heuristics approach to performance science. *Frontiers in Psychology*, 6, 1672.

Rafaeli, A., Barron, G., & Haber, K. (2002). The effects of queue structure on attitudes. *Journal of Service Research*, 5(2), 125–139.

Raz, O., & Ert, E. (2008). "Size Counts": The Effect of Queue Length on Choice between Similar Restaurants. *Advances in Consumer Research*, 35.

Sampson, S. E., & Froehle, C. M. (2006). Foundations and implications of a proposed unified services theory. *Production and Operations Management*, 15(2), 329–343.

Schultz, K. L., McClain, J. O., & Thomas, L. J. (2003). Overcoming the dark side of worker flexibility. *Journal of Operations Management*, 21(1), 81–92.

Siemsen, E., Roth, A. V., Balasubramanian, S., & Anand, G. (2009). The influence of psychological safety and confidence in knowledge on employee knowledge sharing. *Manufacturing & Service Operations Management*, 11(3), 429–447.

Soman, D. (2001). The mental accounting of sunk time costs: Why time is not like money. *J. Behav. Decision Making*, 14, 169–185.

Soman, D., & Shi, M. (2003). Virtual progress: The effect of path characteristics on perceptions of progress and choice. *Management Science*, 49(9), 1229–1250.

Staats, B. R., Brunner, D. J., & Upton, D. M. (2011). Lean principles, learning, and knowledge work: Evidence from a software services provider. *Journal of Operations Management*, 29(5), 376–390.

Staats, B. R., KC, D. S., & Gino, F. (2017). Maintaining beliefs in the face of negative news: The moderating role of experience. *Management Science*.

Sterman, J. D. (1989). Modeling managerial behavior: Misperceptions of feedback in a dynamic decision making experiment. *Management Science*, 35(3), 321–339.

Sterman, J. D., & Dogan, G. (2015). I'm not hoarding, I'm just stocking up before the hoarders get here: Behavioral causes of phantom ordering in supply chains. *Journal of Operations Management*, 39, 6–22.

Su, X. (2008). Bounded rationality in newsvendor models. *Manufacturing & Service Operations Management*, 10(4), 566–589.

Thaler, R. (1985). Mental accounting and consumer choice. *Marketing Science*, 4(3), 199–214.

Tversky, A., & Kahneman, D. (1974). Judgment under uncertainty: Heuristics and biases. *Science*, 185(4157), 1124–1131.

Unzicker, D. K. (1999). The psychology of being put on hold: An exploratory study of service quality. *Psychology & Marketing*, 16(4), 327–350.

Urda, J., & Loch, C. H. (2013). Social preferences and emotions as regulators of behavior in processes. *Journal of Operations Management*, 31(1–2), 6–23.

Van Oyen, M. P., Gel, E. G., & Hopp, W. J. (2001). Performance opportunity for workforce agility in collaborative and noncollaborative work systems. *IIE Transactions*, 33(9), 761–777.

Veeraraghavan, S., & Debo, L. (2009). Joining longer queues: Information externalities in queue choice. *Manufacturing & Service Operations Management*, 11(4), 543–562.

Wuebben, M., & von Wagenheim, F. (2008). Instant customer base analysis: Managerial heuristics often "get it right". *Journal of Marketing*, 72, 82–93.

Yalch, R. F., & Spangenberg, E. R. (2000). The effects of music in a retail setting on real and perceived shopping times. *Journal of Business Research*, 49(2), 139–147.

Yanofsky, N. S. (2013). *The Outer Limits of Reason: What Science, Mathematics, and Logic Cannot Tell Us*. Cambridge, MA: MIT Press.

Zohar, E., Mandelbaum, A., & Shimkin, N. (2002). Adaptive behavior of impatient customers in tele-queues: Theory and empirical support. *Management Science*, 48(4), 566–583.

Zhou, R., & Soman, D. (2008). Consumers' waiting in queues: The role of first-order and second-order justice. *Psychology & Marketing*, 25(3), 262–279.

5   Strategy and measurement

Bridget Louise Riley's *Arrest 2* (1965) welcomes us to the next theme. Its rippling lines shift from black to grey and create a visual illusion that is both delightful and confusing. Riley is one of the foremost exponents of Op(tical) art, abstract works that give the impression of movement, with flashing and vibrating patterns shaping the viewing experience. Riley's expressed aim is to use these abstract depictions to capture rhythms, tempos and contradictions that parallel human experience. She develops meticulous plans for each composition (with preparatory drawings and collage) but it is her assistants who do the work, painting the final canvases. These twin observations, the content of her work trying to capture the inter-play between dynamic forces and the process of her work being a co-ordination between those who do things and those who design and prioritize things, offers a powerful introduction to this chapter where we reflect on how OM engages with the adjacent concepts of strategy.

Like so much else, asking the 'what is it' question does not generate simple answers. The etymology of strategy derives from the Greek *strategos*, meaning 'leading an army' but the core concept typically addresses some combination of setting objectives – typically long(er) rather than short(er)-term – that direct an organization towards its overall goal and engaging with the 'bigger' picture by being detached from (above?) the distractions of day-to-day activities. Of course, as also discussed in previous chapters, a great deal of decision-making is far less formal than simple planning models assume. In fact, as Mintzberg's (1978) seminal work made clear, given most organizations have inertial structures that constrain change, adopt multiple objectives (that are often in conflict) and, serve markets, comply with regulations, etc. that are often inconsistent in the long term, it is more useful to define strategy as "a pattern in a stream of decisions". In this way, it is possible to incorporate strategies that were intended and those emergent strategies that were realized *despite* intentions.[1] Even if we recognize the problematic nature of strategy, and the limits of managerial agency, strategy in theory and practice is predicated on the notion that actors can have some influence over the strategic direction of an organization.

What is operations strategy?

There is no universally accepted definition of operations strategy (OS) but – echoing Mintzberg's seminal contribution to the broader strategy debate – Slack and Lewis' (2014) define OS as 'the total pattern of decisions that shape the long-term capabilities of any type of operation and their contribution to overall strategy, through the reconciliation of market requirements with operations resources'. Hidden in such a definition, however, are the myriad challenges associated with understanding both OS 'content' – which resources, financed how, using which decisions – and 'process' – the way in which operations strategies are (or can be) formulated (Leong et al. 1990; Voss 1995, 2005; Mills et al. 1995). As Wickham Skinner explains in this key passage from his engaging reflections on the emergence of contemporary operations (well, manufacturing[2]) strategy, a key concern and conceptualization of OS is processual:

> [G]et the class to analyze the operating problem(s) in the case and then back up and examine, first, their implicit manufacturing policies and, then, their competitive issues. This analytic process always demonstrated a conflict between the manufacturing policies and the company's competitive strategic situation, which conflict produced the operating problems. Pow! Wow! It was dynamite in the classroom! (Incidentally, these conflicts are as present today – typically in 95% of every company I enter or study – as they were in the 1960s.)
>
> (Skinner 2007, p. 330)

In other words, this view of OS is less concerned with the detailed content of any given operating problems or policies but more about understanding and resolving the process of (mis)alignment between these concerns and the broader competitive strategy of the firm.

Vertical alignment

Since Skinner (1969) first suggested that "manufacturing's" task was to support corporate objectives, the dominant logic for OS (e.g., Wheelwright 1984) has been to present it as a top-down process (Ward and Duray 2000). Consequently, in this idea of vertical alignment, the different levels of strategy (e.g., corporate, business and functional) form part of an assumed hierarchy, with corporate strategy providing the context for business (unit) strategies, and these in turn provide the context for (various) functional strategies.[3] Following Skinner, the majority of (manufacturing) strategy studies have emphasized this idea of OS as process of vertical alignment (Maruchek et al. 1990; Platts and Gregory 1990; Swamidass et al. 2001; Acur et al. 2003; Nielsen-Englyst 2003; Gorm Rytter et al. 2007; Jagoda and Kiridena 2015). Kim and Arnold (1996) for example, investigated "micro-level" OS processes by examining the consistency between manufacturing's competitive priorities, objectives and action plans. Such an approach is often compared to

Hoshin Kanri, a top-down, multi-step strategic planning process via which strategic goals are communicated and then put into action (Witcher and Butterworth 2001). The word Hoshin can be broken into two parts. The literal translation of *ho-* is 'method or form' and of *-shin* is 'shiny needle or compass' so "Hoshin" is translated as "methodology for setting strategic direction". The word *Kanri* can also be broken into two parts. The first part *kan-*, translates into control and *-ri* into reason or logic. Taken altogether, the common translation is "administration or management". As a top-down approach to alignment, the Hoshin Kanri process is predicated on the existence of clear strategic vision and goals articulated for a multi-year period. Then specific objectives can then be defined, with clear advice that managers should avoid selecting too many goals. These are then 'broken down' into sub-goals, across shorter timeframes (i.e., monthly and weekly) then discussed in such a way that everyone has clarity regarding what needs to be accomplished. What is often called a *catchball* system is used as a critical part of Hoshin Kanri. It is an attempt to build multi-directional and regular communication to ensure the development of appropriate targets via a system that actively seeks the opinions of all employees through meetings and interactions. The name derives from a children's game, but instead of a ball, ideas are thrown back and forth. Progress towards these goals is then reviewed on a regular basis, with a larger annual review at the end of the year. There have been a number of company-specific adaptations of Hoshin Kanri including Policy Deployment at AT&T, Managing for Results at Xerox, Policy Management at Florida Power and Light, Hoshin Planning at Hewlett-Packard, etc. Vertical alignment is not only about top-down direction of course, echoing Mintzberg's notion of emergent strategy, it also addresses, the more OM idea, of 'bottom-up' activity, such as operations improvements, cumulatively shaping strategy. Alternative models (laws: by Schmenner and Swink 1998) have been proposed to explain the mechanisms of competition on the basis of these operations capabilities. These models are summarized in Figure 5.1.

The first is the 'trade-off' model which observes that, in simple terms, if one thing increases, another must decrease. Trade-offs emerge from many situations, including physics – for instance, a cargo vessel can carry either a few large items or lots of small items. Given an operation is typically a technologically

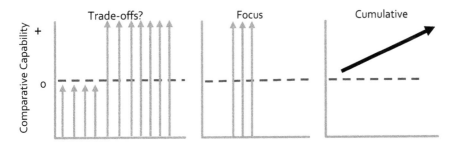

Figure 5.1 Different models (laws) of capability development

constrained entity, finite choices among resources always introduce constraints and choices (Skinner 1996; Boyer and Lewis 2002). In this strategic context, we are most commonly referring to alternative configurations of an operating model, such as the allocation of time and attention towards different tasks. It is observed that over time, those operations that prioritize (resources, etc.) achieving excellence in a few selected performance dimensions will outperform plants that pursue excellence in many dimensions of performance (Skinner 1974/1969). The concept of a trade-off suggests strategic choices made with complete knowledge of the dis/function of each setup, for example, trade-offs exist between lead-times and inventory levels. Quoting Skinner's seminal work at length summarizes the limitations of such an assumption:

> [M]ost managers will readily admit that there are compromises or trade-offs to be made in designing an airplane or a truck. In the case of an airplane, tradeoffs would involve such matters as cruising speed, takeoff and landing distances, initial cost, maintenance, fuel consumption, passenger comfort, and cargo or passenger capacity. A given stage of technology defines limits as to what can be accomplished in these respects. For instance, no one today can design a 500-passenger plane that can land on a carrier and also break the sonic barrier. Much the same thing is true of manufacturing. The variables of cost, time, quality, technological constraints, and customer satisfaction place limits on what management can do, force compromises, and demand an explicit recognition of a multitude of trade-offs and choices. Yet everywhere I find plants which have *inadvertently* emphasized one yardstick at the expense of another, more important one.
>
> (Skinner 1974/1969)

The trade-off between flexibility and efficiency has been of particular attention in OS (e.g., Sawhney 2012; Anand and Ward 2004). Operations often prioritize cost and time savings – with their corresponding short-term benefits but some firms seem to have "ambidextrous" traits that help them better balance this relationship. This mediation is central to discussions of mass customization. BMW, for example, is highly flexible in developing entirely new market segments (electric cars, Mini, etc.), but, by producing many of its cars "to order" using modular vehicle architectures and an advanced configuration system, it can also produce and deliver customized cars at a relatively competitive cost. Kortmann et al. (2014) extend this logic and present different categories of ambidextrous OS. For some firms (such as VW and Nike) who have grown over extended periods, have loyal customers and strong brands, etc., innovation risk can be diversified over multiple projects, and profitability underpins investment in mass customization technologies. Alternatively, some operations who face declining/unprofitable markets, lack brand strength, switching customers, etc. concentrate investments on ambidextrous innovation capabilities to rapidly enter new product markets, without developing mass customization capabilities.

Another contemporary set of reflections on trade-offs emerge from discussion of the process management triangle (Klassen and Menor 2007); a heuristic identifying a trade-off relationship between Capacity utilization, Variability, and Inventory (Lovejoy 1998). The implication of the CVI trade-off is that performance is improved through either more 'buffer' capacity (i.e., lower capacity utilization), reduced variability (more information can be a substitute for variability reduction) or more 'buffer' inventory.

The second related (consequential?) concept is that of focus. Once again it was Skinner (1974) who observed, during another study of factories in a variety of industries, that those focusing on a limited set of tasks were more productive than similar factories attempting a broader array of tasks. Similar assertions have been made in service settings to the point that the benefits of focus are now essentially 'received wisdom' in OM (cf. the famous Shouldice Hospital case, Southwest Airlines use of the Boeing 737, etc.). The benefits of focus, establishing the optimal scope of operations and the benefits of operational specialization, is in part revisiting aspects of the OM 'origins story' (Smith's (1776) pin factory, etc.), but these early arguments rest largely on individual worker performance and the benefits of individual specialization may not translate to a higher level of organization. Focus will influence a wide range of OS decisions – from hiring to Make v Buy to capacity growth to technology investments, etc. – and impact a range of performance dimensions including quality, productivity, satisfaction, etc. in both manufacturing (e.g., Fisher and Ittner 1999) and service (e.g., Huckman and Zinner 2008) context. OM research generally supports the benefits of focus (Tsikriktsis 2007; Huckman and Zinner 2008) and there is a strong logic for the benefits, such as the static economies of scale that appear as either reductions in average cost via amortizing of fixed investments or improvements in average quality from learning, depth of know-how, etc. There may also be benefits in 'related spillovers'; Fong Boh et al. (2007) for example, found that software team productivity was more strongly impacted by the group's average experience with *related* activities than average experience with the focal activity.

Despite this, some scholars have noted that there are unfocused operations that seem to achieve high levels of operational performance (Ketokivi and Jokinen 2006)? Similarly, authors (e.g., O'Reilly and Tushman 2004) have suggested that more focused organizations may face additional challenges when innovating. In one of the most comprehensive recent assessments of focus, Clark and Huckman (2012), who investigate in a US hospital setting whether an operating unit that is more focused on a given activity achieves higher quality performance compared to a less-focused unit engaged in the same activity (cf. KC and Terwiesch 2011), ask whether a focused operating unit can be "too focused"? Their findings – after controlling for the effect of "cherry picking" easy-to-treat patients[4] – suggest that the benefits of specializing may depend on the degree to which the unit "cospecializes" in related activities; providing a potential explanation for why there can be limits to (narrow) focus.

The third influential model is that of 'cumulative' capabilities. Rather than focusing on specific capabilities, operations can, and therefore should, be developed along multiple dimensions simultaneously (Ferdows and De Meyer 1990). The argument is that certain capabilities such as quality are fundamental and consequently enable improvements to be made more easily in other capabilities such as cost and then flexibility, etc. The specific trajectories (and indeed the actual list of capabilities: Avella et al. (2011) amongst several authors including sustainability in their analysis) of this cumulative improvement process has been extensively debated (Schroeder et al. 2011; Narasimhan and Schoenherr 2013, etc.).

Although these models are often presented as opposing laws, Schmenner and Swink (1998) argue that they are theoretically complementary rather than substitutes. They explain that although certain proponents of "Japanese management and World Class Manufacturing" cited evidence of firms that do indeed lead their competitors in almost every dimension of performance, the law of trade-offs is reflected in comparisons across plants at a given point in time, whereas the law of cumulative capabilities is reflected in improvement within individual plants over time and thus the two approaches are not in conflict. This remains an important area of discussion and debate: the dialogue between Singh et al. (2015) and Sarmiento et al. (2018) being of particular interest/relevance. Related discussions can also be found in the 50+ articles (Hitt et al. 2016) that apply Resource-Based Theory (RBT) to OS. Although often treated as synonyms (tangible and intangible), resources are perhaps best conceived as the building blocks that are bundled together, or orchestrated (e.g., Craighead et al. 2009; Grewal and Slotegraaf 2007) to create capabilities (Sirmon et al. 2011).

Ultimately, presenting top-down or bottom-up as a dichotomy is unlikely to apply in practice. Kim et al. (2014) for example, propose an integrated process model of OS formation that addresses both top-down and bottom-up perspectives. They also suggest an important contingency on this interaction, the extent to which organizational structure is centralized or decentralized. This provides a useful link to the next section, where we explore the horizontal/structural aspects of OS.

Horizontal alignment

OS is typically understood to be one of a series of functional strategies, such as marketing, R&D and sales, that should in theory be coherent with each other. This idea of horizontal alignment is another key aspect of OS. The catchball part of the Hoshin Kanri process is in part aimed at addressing the different perspectives that emerge in cross-functional settings. This horizontal dynamic also introduces some fascinating behavioural elements, many related to the challenges of process coordination and control described in previous chapters. More specifically, such collaborations are replete with various social dilemmas (cf. McCarter and Northcraft 2007). A social dilemma is not about knowing which fork and knife to use at a posh restaurant, but rather those situations where an individual (or function, etc.) must choose between doing what is in their own best interest or the group's best interest (i.e., share all information or retain some key insights, maximize local and short-term performance measures or look to increase total system performance, etc.). OS, like all strategy, is largely a political process, involving coalition building, bargaining, and conflict resolution among representatives of these subunits. We know from the group research discussed in the previous chapter that people care about payoffs in the context of other members of their environment (Loch and Wu 2008) and, with specific reference to measurement and comparison, people are motivated by "relative payoffs that represent social status, they care about reciprocity and fairness that characterize social relationships, and they care about group identity" (Urda and Loch 2013). Such group identity concerns can be particularly significant in a strategy development and implementation setting where professional and inter-professional identities are being challenged. Social dilemmas are those situations where being uncooperative can be beneficial at the partner's expense – unless all partners also choose to be uncooperative, in which case no one benefits. In other words, many horizontal aspects of OS speak to both our better and worst natures and can frequently create prisoner's dilemma type situations. Moreover, this kind of opportunistic behaviour, and hence the incentive to behave in that way, increases when, for example, people/functions/units have very different specialized skills and knowledge.

Directly related to discussion of horizontal (and vertical) aspects of OS process (Boyer et al. 2005; Swink and Way 1995) is the discussion of OS content: what subjects, decisions, technologies, etc. are included in this sub-strategy.

The 'content' of operations strategy?

Although different scholars refer to them in slightly different ways, including 'decision areas', 'policy areas', 'sub-strategies' or 'tasks', a great deal of research explores different aspects of OS content. From consideration of the (dis)economic scale of capacity and the timing of any changes (Hayes and Wheelwright 1984; Olhager et al. 2001), to the set of broad and long-term decisions governing how the operation is improved on a continuing basis (e.g., Six Sigma: Linderman et al. 2003), any larger, longer lead-time, decisions (i.e., more existential, capital intensive/complex investments, etc.) are of interest to OS researchers. For example, the *Make* (or more accurately Do) *versus Buy* (MvB) decision (de Treville et al. 2017) is a foundational concern (Stock and Tatikonda 2000; McIvor 2009). It is the decision that sets the boundaries on what constitutes an operations internal/external resources, capabilities, etc. (Leiblein et al. 2002). The MvB literature has evolved from its original 'transaction cost economics' roots (i.e., make when faced with high transaction cost situations) to address more strategic considerations such as the protection and development of resources (skills, knowledge and technologies) and capabilities (Nellore and Söderquist 2000; Holcomb and Hitt 2007) and supply risks (McIvor 2008). Interestingly, one or two notable exceptions (e.g., Mantel et al. 2006), the behavioural and processual aspects of decision-making regarding specific OS content has received more limited attention despite its alignment with much of the behavioural economics field.

Measurement and (operations) strategy

Metrics and measurement (of activities, outputs, variance, etc.) is widely understood to provide the foundation for operational control and, via increased transparency (Bernstein 2012; Buell 2016), organizational learning. Melnyk et al. (2004), quoting manufacturing and management consultant Oliver Wight, offer the maxim, "You get what you inspect, not what you expect". Neely et al. (1995) defined performance measurement as using metrics to quantify the efficiency and/ or effectiveness of action and Melnyk et al. (2014) defined performance management as the process for developing the metric set, setting goals, collecting, analysing, reporting, interpreting and assessing performance differentials. Of course, such processes are an omni-present part of modern operational life; with contemporary best practice – from call centre to production cell to agile software team – designed to support the observability of work. The seventh principle of the Toyota Way is to "use visual control so no problems are hidden" (Liker 2004, pp. 149–158). Similarly, research into high-performance workplaces (Appelbaum and Batt 1993; Ichniowski and Shaw 1999) suggests accurate perceptions regarding the link between actions, performance (and rewards) is a critical component of effectiveness. Accurate measurement and reporting also underpin many of the key TQM practices discussed in previous chapters, which, again, target simultaneous learning and control (Sitkin et al. 1994). Consequently, measurement had been a long-term interest to OM practice and research (Leong and Ward 1995; Neely et al. 1995, and New and Szwejczewski 1995, etc.). Consider the work of Henry L. Gantt, the management consultant and business guru who spent several years (1887–1893) working with F.W. Taylor applying scientific management principles at Midvale and Bethlehem Steel. He is best known for his eponymous visual charts,[5] "a method of scheduling and recording work" (1903). Similarly, in his 1916 book *Work, Wages, and Profits*, he proposed that the foreman (sic) needs a daily "order of work" and needs to coordinate activities to avoid "interferences". Intriguingly, he also frequently observed that some of the most elegant schedules created by planning offices were useless if ignored.

The importance of measurement to (operations) strategy has also been long recognized (Bourne et al. 2000; Franco-Santos et al. 2012; Koufteros et al. 2014; Chatha and Butt 2015; Bititci et al. 2018; Micheli and Mura 2017). Melnyk et al. (2004) refer to the orchestrating role of performance measurement systems that are "ultimately responsible for maintaining alignment and coordination" (p. 213). This echoes the logic introduced at the start of the chapter, that the (functional) strategy (process) is in large part about aligning actions, resources, employee behaviours, etc. with an organization's mission and strategic objectives. Such (vertical and horizontal) alignment typically depends on managers "convey[ing] the strategy to everyone else in terms they can understand, thus making the strategy concrete and meaningful" (Melnyk et al. 2014, p. 173). This translation task is a fundamental aspect of the Hoshin Kanri approach to strategy 'deployment' mentioned earlier. Equally, information needs to flow 'up' the hierarchy else localized problem solving has no impact on organization-wide learning (Tucker et al. 2002).

Various authors have focused on the relationships between strategy and performance measurement (Micheli and Manzoni 2010) with a positive impact on strategic alignment found at both organizational and business unit levels. Similar conclusions were drawn at the individual level, including explicit recognition of the psychological mechanisms involved. Malina and Selto (2015) for example, argue that performance information can act as a managerial 'nudge' and, similarly, Franco-Santos et al. (2012) found it to be an effective mechanism for:

> [E]ngaging managers in the strategy formulation and review processes, enabling the strategy to be implemented as it facilitates the translation of strategy into operational terms, encouraging managers to embrace the organisation's strategy as a continuous process rather than a one-off exercise, and improving strategic alignment, i.e., helping organisations align their actions in pursuit of their strategic objectives.

Concluding comments

There are reasons to be sceptical that ever more sophisticated measurement offers a strategic panacea. As Bernstein (2012) notes there are multiple well-documented instances in which greater "measurement" has encouraged hiding behaviours, producing only the appearance of alignment, learning and control. Dalton (1959, p. 47) described how managers, mandated by their superiors to conduct "surprise inspections", instead chose to "telephone various heads before a given inspection telling them the starting point, time, and route that would be followed" so that each inspection would simply "appear to catch the chiefs off-guard". Roy (1952) and Burawoy (1979), in reconfirming the "restriction of output" observed in the Bank Wiring Observation Room at the Hawthorne Works (Mayo 1933; Roethlisberger and Dickson 1939), provided substantial detail on the "quota restriction" and "goldbricking" activities in the Greer machine shop (Roy 1952), which only became worse when managers were in sight. Subsequent insider tales from one of General Motors' largest and most open plants portrayed management's stance on various workarounds like "doubling up" as "a simple matter of see no evil, hear no evil", leaving workers with the challenge of hiding their self-defined "scams" within the context of an observable factory floor – the more observable the factory floor, the more effort "wasted" on hiding them (Hamper 1986, pp. xix, 35). Each of those facilities was designed to be extremely transparent, yet those organization designs with high observability resulted not in accurate observability but, rather, only in an "illusion of transparency" (Gilovich et al. 1998) – a myth of control and learning – maintained through careful group-level behavioural responses by those being observed. Although observability was achieved through the removal of physical barriers like walls, accurate observability (transparency) was not. Analogously, increasing observability in a factory may in fact reduce transparency, which is displaced by illusory transparency and a myth of learning and control, by triggering increasingly hard-to-detect hiding behaviours – a result Bernstein terms the "transparency paradox".

Notes

1 Mintzberg and Waters (1985) further elaborated this conception of deliberate and emergent strategies as two ends of a continuum by identifying various types of strategies including what they labelled planned, entrepreneurial, ideological, umbrella, process, unconnected, consensus and imposed.
2 OS, like most of OM, has its roots in analysis of manufacturing activity, hence a lot of the literature in this area refers to Manufacturing Strategy.
3 Given this framing logic, there has also been a skew towards larger operations as the focus for OS. Some studies include SMEs as case studies (Swamidass et al. 2001; Kiridena et al. 2009) but this is rarely considered as an explicit variable. A notable exception being Barnes's work (2001, 2002a, 2002b) analyzing manufacturing strategy formulation and implementation in UK SMEs. This is a broader concern with the OM literature, many of the problems identified and solutions proposed assume a level of endogenous complexity, scale, resource, longevity, etc. that many SMEs do not have? (cf. Cagliano et al. 2001, etc.).
4 In the celebrated Shouldice hospital case study, this 'cherry picking' of specific types of patient is central to the design of the operating/business model.
5 It is worth noting that he also argued that businesses have societal obligations, and in a precursor of more contemporary quality management, developed an incentive system that linked managerial bonuses to how well employees improved performance.

References

Acur, N., Gertsen, F., Sun, H., & Frick, J. (2003). The formalisation of manufacturing strategy and its influence on the relationship between competitive objectives, improvement goals, and action plans. *International Journal of Operations & Production Management*, 23(10), 1114–1141.

Adler, P. S., & Clark, K. B. (1991). Behind the learning curve: A sketch of the learning process. *Management Science*, 37(3), 267–281.

Anand, G., & Gray, J. V. (2017). Strategy and organization research in operations management. *Journal of Operations Management*, 53, 1–8.

Anand, G., & Ward, P. T. (2004). Fit, flexibility and performance in manufacturing: Coping with dynamic environments. *Production and Operations Management*, 13(4), 369–385.

Appelbaum, E., & Batt, R. (1993). *High-Performance Work Systems: American Models of Workplace Transformation*. Public Interest Publications, Arlington, VA 22210.

Atasu, A., Sarvary, M., & Van Wassenhove, L. N. (2008). Remanufacturing as a marketing strategy. *Management Science*, 54(10), 1731–1746.

Avella, L., Vazquez-Bustelo, D., & Fernandez, E. (2011). Cumulative manufacturing capabilities: An extended model and new empirical evidence. *International Journal of Production Research*, 49(3), 707–729.

Bargh, J. A., Chen, M., & Burrows, L. (1996). Automaticity of social behavior: Direct effects of trait construct and stereotype activation on action. *Journal of Personality and Social Psychology*, 71(2), 230.

Barnes, D. (2001). Research methods for the empirical investigation of the process of formation of operations strategy. *International Journal of Operations & Production Management*, 21(8), 1076–1095.

Barnes, D. (2002a). The complexities of the manufacturing strategy formation process in practice. *International Journal of Operations & Production Management*, 22(10), 1090–1111.

Barnes, D. (2002b). The manufacturing strategy formation process in small and medium-sized enterprises. *Journal of Small Business and Enterprise Development*, 9(2), 130–149.

Bendoly, E. (2016). Fit, bias, and enacted sensemaking in data visualization: Frameworks for continuous development in operations and supply chain management analytics. *Journal of Business Logistics*, 37(1), 6–17.

Bendoly, E., Croson, R., Goncalves, P., & Schultz, K. (2010). Bodies of knowledge for research in behavioral operations. *Production and Operations Management*, 19(4), 434–452.

Bendoly, E., Donohue, K., & Schultz, K. L. (2006). Behavior in operations management: Assessing recent findings and revisiting old assumptions. *Journal of Operations Management*, 24(6), 737–752.

Bernstein, E. S. (2012). The transparency paradox: A role for privacy in organizational learning and operational control. *Administrative Science Quarterly*, 57(2), 181–216.

Bertel, S., & Kirlik, A. (2010). Fast and frugal heuristics. In *Wiley Encyclopedia of Operations Research and Management Science*, Wiley.

Bititci, U. S., Bourne, M., Cross, J. A., Nudurupati, S. S., & Sang, K. (2018). Towards a theoretical foundation for performance measurement and management. *International Journal of Management Reviews*, 20(3), 653–660.

Boudreau, J., Hopp, W., McClain, J. O., Thomas, L. J. (2003). On the interface between operations and human resource management. *Manufacturing and Service Operations Management*, 5(3), 179–202.

Bourne, M., Mills, J., Wilcox, M., Neely, A., & Platts, K. (2000). Designing, implementing and updating performance measurement systems. *International Journal of Operations & Production Management*, 20(7), 754–771.

Bowen, D. E., & Schneider, B. (1985). Boundary spanning role employees and the service encounter: Some guidelines for management research. In J. A. Czepiel, M. R. Soloman, & C. F. Surprenant (eds.), *The Service Encounter*. Lexington, MA: Lexington Books.

Boyer, K. K., & Lewis, M. W. (2002). Competitive priorities: Investigating the need for trade-offs in operations strategy. *Production and Operations Management*, 11(1), 9–20.

Boyer, K. K., Swink, M., & Rosenzweig, E. D. (2005). Operations strategy research in the POMS journal. *Production and Operations Management*, 14(4), 442–449.

Bozarth, C., & McDermott, C. (1998). Configurations in manufacturing strategy: A review and directions for future research. *Journal of Operations Management*, 16(4), 427–439.

Brown, K. A. (2000). Predicting safe employee behaviour in the steel industry: The development and test of a socio-technical model. *Journal of Operations Management*, 18(4), 445–468.

Buell, R. W., Kim, T., & Tsay, C. J. (2016). Creating reciprocal value through operational transparency. *Management Science*, 63(6), 1673–1695.

Burawoy, M. (1979). The anthropology of industrial work. *Annual Review of Anthropology*, 8(1), 231–266.

Cagliano, R., Blackmon, K., & Voss, C. (2001). Small firms under MICROSCOPE: International differences in production/operations management practices and performance. *Integrated Manufacturing Systems*, 12(7), 469–482.

Camerer, C. (1999). Behavioral economics: Reunifying psychology and economics. *Proceedings of the National Academy of Sciences of the United States of America*, 96, 10575–10577.

Chatha, K. A., & Butt, I. (2015). Themes of study in manufacturing strategy literature. *International Journal of Operations & Production Management*, 35(4), 604–698.

Chatha, K. A., Butt, I., & Tariq, A. (2015). Research methodologies and publication trends in manufacturing strategy: A content analysis based literature review. *International Journal of Operations & Production Management*, 35(4), 487–546.

Clark, J. R., & Huckman, R. S. (2012). Broadening focus: Spillovers, complementarities, and specialization in the hospital industry. *Management Science*, 58(4), 708–722.

Craighead, C. W., Hult, G. T. M., & Ketchen Jr, D. J. (2009). The effects of innovation–cost strategy, knowledge, and action in the supply chain on firm performance. *Journal of Operations Management*, 27(5), 405–421.

Croson, R., & Donohue, K. (2006). Behavioral causes of the bullwhip effect and the observed value of inventory information. *Management Science*, 52(3), 323–336.

Croson, R., Schultz, K., Siemsen, E., & Yeo, M. L. (2013). Behavioral operations: The state of the field. *Journal of Operations Management*, 31(1–2), 1–5.

Dalton, M. (1959). *Men who manage: Fusions of feeling and theory in administration.* (2017). New York and London: Routledge.

Dean Jr, J. W., & Bowen, D. E. (1994). Management theory and total quality: Improving research and practice through theory development. *Academy of Management Review*, 19(3), 392–418.

Demeester, L., De Meyer, A., & Grahovac, J. (2014). The role of operations executives in strategy making. *Journal of Operations Management*, 32(7–8), 403–413.

de Treville, S., Ketokivi, M., & Singhal, V. R. (2017). Competitive manufacturing in a high-cost environment: Introduction to the special issue. *Journal of Operations Management*.

Doerr, K. H., & KR Gue. (2013). A performance metric and goal-setting procedure for deadline-oriented processes. *Production and Operations Management*, 22(3), 726–738.

Drake, D. F., Kleindorfer, P. R., & Van Wassenhove, L. N. (2016). Technology choice and capacity portfolios under emissions regulation. *Production and Operations Management*, 25(6), 1006–1025.

Ellway, B. (2016). Design vs practice: How problematic call routing and rerouting restructures the call centre service system. *International Journal of Operations & Production Management*, 36(4), 408–428.

Ferdows, K., & De Meyer, A. (1990). Lasting improvements in manufacturing performance: In search of a new theory. *Journal of Operations Management*, 9(2), 168–184.

Fisher, M. L., & Ittner, C. D. (1999). The impact of product variety on automobile assembly operations: Empirical evidence and simulation analysis. *Management Sci.*, 45(6), 771–786.

Fong Boh, W., Slaughter, S. A., & Espinosa, J. A. (2007). Learning from experience in software development: A multilevel analysis. *Management Science*, 53(8), 1315–1331.

Franco-Santos, M., Lucianetti, L., & Bourne, M. (2012). Contemporary performance measurement systems: A review of their consequences and a framework for research. *Management Accounting Research*, 23(2), 79–119.

Gantt, H.L., (1903). A graphical daily balance in manufacture. *ASME Transactions*, 24, 1322–1336.

Gigerenzer, G., & Gaissmaier, W. (2011). Heuristic decision making. *Annu. Rev. Psychol.*, 62, 451–482.

Gigerenzer, G., & Goldstein, D. G. (1996). Reasoning the fast and frugal way: Models of bounded rationality. *Psychol. Rev.*, 103, 650–669.

Gino, F., & Pisano, G. (2008). Toward a theory of behavioral operations. *Manufacturing & Service Operations Management*, 10(4), 676–691.

Giordani da Silveira, W., Pinheiro de Lima, E., Gouvea da Costa, S. E., & Deschamps, F. (2017). Guidelines for hoshin kanri implementation: Development and discussion. *Production Planning & Control*, 28(10), 843–859.

Gilovich, T., Savitsky, K., & Medvec, V. H. (1998). The illusion of transparency: biased assessments of others' ability to read one's emotional states. *Journal of Personality and Social Psychology*, 75(2), 332.

Gorm Rytter, N., Boer, H., & Koch, C. (2007). Conceptualizing operations strategy processes. *International Journal of Operations & Production Management*, 27(10), 1093–1114.

Grewal, R., & Slotegraaf, R. J. (2007). Embeddedness of organizational capabilities. *Decision Sciences*, 38(3), 451–488.

Hamper, B. (1986). *Rivethead: Tales from the assembly line*. New York, NY: Warner Books.

Hayes, R. H., & Pisano, G. P. (1994). Beyond world-class: The new manufacturing strategy. *Harvard Business Review*, 72(1), 77–86.

Hayes, R. H., & Wheelwright, S. C. (1984). *Restoring our competitive edge: competing through manufacturing*. New York, NY: John Wiley & Sons.

Hitt, M. A., Xu, K., & Carnes, C. M. (2016). Resource based theory in operations management research. *Journal of Operations Management*, 41, 77–94.

Holcomb, T. R., & Hitt, M. A. (2007). Toward a model of strategic outsourcing. *Journal of Operations Management*, 25(2), 464–481.

Huckman, R., & Zinner, D. (2008). Does focus improve operational performance? Lessons from the management of clinical trials. *Strategic Management J.*, 29(2), 173–193.

Ichniowski, C., & Shaw, K. (1999). The effects of human resource management systems on economic performance: An international comparison of US and Japanese plants. *Management Science*, 45(5), 704–721.

Jagoda, K., & Kiridena, S. (2015). Operations strategy processes and performance: Insights from the contract apparel manufacturing industry. *Journal of Manufacturing Technology Management*, 26(2), 261–279.

Kahneman, D., Slovic, P., & Tversky, A. (1982). *Judgment Under Uncertainty: Heuristics and Biases*. Cambridge, UK: Cambridge University Press.

Katsikopoulos, K. V. (2011). Psychological heuristics for making inferences: Definition, performance, and the emerging theory and practice. *Decision Analysis*, 8(1), 10–29.

Katsikopoulos, K. V., & Gigerenzer, G. (2013). Behavioral operations management: A blind spot and a research program. *Journal of Supply Chain Management*, 49(1), 3–7.

Kaufmann, L., Michel, A., & Carter, C. R. (2009). Debiasing strategies in supply management decision making. *Journal of Business Logistics*, 30(1), 85–106.

KC, D. S., & Terwiesch, C. (2011). The effects of focus on performance: Evidence from California hospitals. *Management Sci.*, 57(11), 1897–1912.

Kelman, M. G. (2011). *The Heuristics Debate*. New York, NY: Oxford University Press.

Ketokivi, M., & Jokinen, M. (2006). Strategy, uncertainty and the focused factory in international process manufacturing. *Journal of Operations Management*, 24(3), 250–270.

Kim, J. S., & Arnold, P. (1996). Operationalizing manufacturing strategy: an exploratory study of constructs and linkage. *International Journal of Operations & Production Management*, 16(12), 45–73.

Kim, Y. H., Sting, F. J., & Loch, C. H. (2014). Top-down, bottom-up, or both? Toward an integrative perspective on operations strategy formation. *Journal of Operations Management*, 32(7–8), 462–474.

Kiridena, S., Hasan, M., & Kerr, R. (2009). Exploring deeper structures in manufacturing strategy formation processes: a qualitative inquiry. *International Journal of Operations & Production Management*, 29(4), 386–417.

Klassen, R. D., & Menor, L. J. (2007). The process management triangle: An empirical investigation of process trade-offs. *Journal of Operations Management*, 25(5), 1015–1034.

Kortmann, S., Gelhard, C., Zimmermann, C., & Piller, F. T. (2014). Linking strategic flexibility and operational efficiency: The mediating role of ambidextrous operational capabilities. *Journal of Operations Management*, 32(7–8), 475–490.

Kotha, S., & Orne, D. (1989). Generic Manufacturing Strategies: A Conceptual Synthesis. *Strategic Management Journal*, 10(3), 211–231.

Koufteros, X., Verghese, A. J., & Lucianetti, L. (2014). The effect of performance measurement systems on firm performance: A cross-sectional and a longitudinal study. *Journal of Operations Management*, 32(6), 313–336.

Leiblein, M. J., Reuer, J. J., & Dalsace, F. (2002). Do make or buy decisions matter? The influence of organizational governance on technological performance. *Strategic Management Journal*, 23(9), 817–833.

Leong, G. K., Snyder, D. L., & Ward, P. T. (1990). Research in the process and content of manufacturing strategy. *Omega*, 18(2), 109–122.

Leong, G.K. & Ward, P. T. (1995). The six Ps of manufacturing strategy. *International Journal of Operations & Production Management*, 15(12), 32–45.

Levinthal, D. A. (2011). A behavioral approach to strategy: What's the alternative? *Strategic Management Journal*, 32(13), 1517–1523.

Liker, J. K. (2004). *The Toyota Way*. McGraw Hill, New York, NY.

Linderman, K., Schroeder, K. R., Choo, A. S. (2006). Six Sigma: The role of goals in improvement teams. *Journal of Operations Management*, 24(6), 779–790.

Linderman, K., Schroeder, R. G., Zaheer, S., & Choo, A. S. (2003). Six Sigma: A goal-theoretic perspective. *Journal of Operations Management*, 21(2), 193–203.

Loch, C., & Wu, Y. (2005). Behavioral operations management. *Foundations and Trends in Technology, Information, and Operations Management*, 1(3), 121–232.

Loch, C., & Wu, Y. (2008). Social preferences and supply chain performance: An experimental study. *Management Science*, 54(11), 1835–1849.

Löfving, M., Säfsten, K., & Winroth, M. (2016). Manufacturing strategy formulation, leadership style and organisational culture in small and medium-sized enterprises. *International Journal of Manufacturing Technology and Management*, 30(5), 306–325.

Lopes, L. L. (1991). The rhetoric of irrationality. *Theory and Psychology*, 1(1), 65–82.

Lovejoy, W. S. (1998). Integrated operations: A proposal for operations management teaching and research. *Production and Operations Management*, 7(2), 106–124.

Malina, M. A., & Selto, F. H. (2015). Behavioral-economic nudges and performance measurement models. *Journal of Management Accounting Research*, 27, 27–45.

Mantel, S. P., Tatikonda, M. V., & Liao, Y. (2006). A behavioral study of supply manager decision-making: Factors influencing make versus buy evaluation. *Journal of Operations Management*, 24(6), 822–838.

Marginson, D. E. W., McAulay, L., Roush, M., & van Zijl, T. (2014). A positive psychological role for performance measures? *Management Accounting Research*, 25(1), 63–75.

Marucheck, A., Pannesi, R., & Anderson, C. (1990). An exploratory study of the manufacturing strategy process in practice. *Journal of Operations Management*, 9(1), 101–123.

Mayo E. (1933). *The human problems of an industrial civilization*. New York, NY: Macmillan.

McCarter, M. W., & Northcraft, G. B. (2007). Happy together?: Insights and implications of viewing managed supply chains as a social dilemma. *Journal of Operations Management*, 25(2), 498–511.

McIvor, R. (2008). What is the right outsourcing strategy for your process?. *European Management Journal*, 26(1), 24–34.

McIvor, R. (2009). How the transaction cost and resource-based theories of the firm inform outsourcing evaluation. *Journal of Operations Management*, 27(1), 45–63.

Melnyk, S. A., Bititci, U., Platts, K., Tobias, J., & Andersen, B. (2014). Is performance measurement and management fit for the future? *Management Accounting Research*, 25(2), 173–186.

Melnyk, S. A., Hanson, J., & Calantone, R. (2010). Hitting the target . . . but missing the point: Resolving the paradox of strategic transition. *Long Range Planning*, 43(4), 555–574.

Melnyk, S. A., Stewart, D. M., & Swink, M. (2004). Metrics and performance measurement in operations management: Dealing with the metrics maze. *Journal of Operations Management*, 22(3), 209–218.

Micheli, P., & Manzoni, J.-F. (2010). Strategic performance measurement: Benefits, limits and paradoxes. *Long Range Planning*, 43(4), 465–476.

Micheli, P., & Mura, M. (2017). Executing strategy through comprehensive performance measurement systems. *International Journal of Operations & Production Management*, 37(4), 423–443.

Miller, J. G., & Roth, A. V. (1994). A taxonomy of manufacturing strategies. *Management Science*, 40(3), 285–304.

Mills, J., Platts, K. and Gregory, M. (1995), "A framework for the design of manufacturing strategy processes: a contingency approach", *International Journal of Operations & Production Management*, Vol. 15 No. 4, pp. 17–49.

Mintzberg, H. (1978). Patterns in strategy formation. *Management Science*, 24(9), 934–948.

Mintzberg, H., & Waters, J. A. (1985). Of strategies, deliberate and emergent. *Strategic Management Journal*, 6(3), 257–272.

Narasimhan, R., & Schoenherr, T. (2013). Revisiting the progression of competitive capabilities: Results from a repeated cross-sectional investigation. *International Journal of Production Research*, 51(22), 6631–6650.

Neely, A., Gregory, M., & Platts, K. (1995). Performance measurement system design: a literature review and research agenda. *International Journal of Operations & Production Management*, 15(4), 80–116.

Nielsen-Englyst, L. (2003). Operations strategy formation: a continuous process. *Integrated Manufacturing Systems*, 14(8), 677–685.

Nellore, R., & Söderquist, K. (2000). Strategic outsourcing through specifications. *Omega*, 28(5), 525–540.

New, C. C., & Szwejczewski, M. (1995). Performance measurement and the focused factory: empirical evidence. *International Journal of Operations & Production Management*, 15(4), 63–79.

Olhager, J., & Feldmann, A. (2018). Distribution of manufacturing strategy decision-making in multi-plant networks. *International Journal of Production Research*, 56(1–2), 692–708.

Olhager, J., Rudberg, M., & Wikner, J. (2001). Long-term capacity management: Linking the perspectives from manufacturing strategy and sales and operations planning. *International Journal of Production Economics*, 69(2), 215–225.

O'Reilly 3rd, C. A., & Tushman, M. L. (2004). *The ambidextrous organization*. Harvard Business Review, 82(4), 74.

Phadnis, S. S., Sheffi, Y., Caplice, C., & Singh, M. (2017). Strategic cognition of operations executives. *Production and Operations Management*, 26(12), 2323–2337.

Platts, K. W., & Gregory, M. J. (1990). Manufacturing audit in the process of strategy formulation. *International Journal of Operations & Production Management*, 10(9), 5–26.

Pulles, N. J., & Hartman, P. (2017). Likeability and its effect on outcomes of interpersonal interaction. *Industrial Marketing Management*, 66, 56–63.

Raab, M., & Gigerenzer, G. (2015). The power of simplicity: A fast-and-frugal heuristics approach to performance science. *Frontiers in Psychology*, 6, 1672.

Roethlisberger, F. J., & Dickson, W. J. (2003). *Management and the Worker (Vol. 5)*. Hove: Psychology Press.

Roy, D. (1952). Quota restriction and goldbricking in a machine shop. *American Journal of Sociology*, 57(5), 427–442.

Sarmiento, R., Whelan, G., & Thürer, M. (2018). A note on "beyond the trade-off and cumulative capabilities models: Alternative models of operations strategy". *International Journal of Production Research*, 56(12), 4368–4375.

Sawhney, R. (2012). Implementing labor flexibility: A missing link between acquired labor flexibility and plant performance. *Journal of Operations Management*, 31(1–2), 98–108.

Schmenner, R. W., & Swink, M. L. (1998). On theory in operations management. *Journal of Operations Management*, 17(1), 97–113.

Schroeder, R. G., Shah, R., & Xiaosong Peng, D. (2011). The cumulative capability "sand cone" model revisited: A new perspective for manufacturing strategy. *International Journal of Production Research*, 49(16), 4879–4901.

Schultz, K. L., McClain, J. O., & Thomas, L. J. (2003). Overcoming the dark side of worker flexibility. *Journal of Operations Management*, 21(1), 81–92.

Singh, P. J., Wiengarten, F., Nand, A. A., & Betts, T. (2015). Beyond the trade-off and cumulative capabilities models: Alternative models of operations strategy. *International Journal of Production Research*, 53(13), 4001–4020.

Sirmon, D. G., Hitt, M. A., Ireland, R. D., & Gilbert, B. A. (2011). Resource orchestration to create competitive advantage: Breadth, depth, and life cycle effects. *Journal of Management*, 37(5), 1390–1412.

Sitkin, S. B., Sutcliffe, K. M., & Schroeder, R. G. (1994). Distinguishing control from learning in total quality management: a contingency perspective. *Academy of Management Review*, 19(3), 537–564.

Skinner, W. (1969). Manufacturing-missing link in corporate strategy, *Harvard Business Review*, May–June.

Skinner, W. (1974). The focused factory. *Harv. Bus. Rev.*, May–June, pp. 113–121.

Skinner, W. (1996). Manufacturing strategy on the "S" curve. *Production and Operations Management*, 5(1), 3–14.

Skinner, W. (2007). Manufacturing strategy: the story of its evolution. *Journal of Operations Management*, 25(2), 328–335.

Slack, N. & Lewis, M. (2014). *Operations strategy*. Pearson Education.

Smith, A. (1776). *An Inquiry into the Nature and Causes of the Wealth of Nations*, University of Chicago Press; UK ed. edition (1977).

Stock, G. N., & Tatikonda, M. V. (2000). A typology of project-level technology transfer processes. *Journal of Operations Management*, 18(6), 719–737.

Staats, B. R., Brunner, D. J., & Upton, D. M. (2011). Lean principles, learning, and knowledge work: Evidence from a software services provider. *Journal of Operations Management*, 29(5), 376–390.

Staats, B. R., KC, D. S., & Gino, F. (2017). Maintaining beliefs in the face of negative news: The moderating role of experience. *Management Science*.

Sterman, J. D., & Dogan, G. (2015). I'm not hoarding, I'm just stocking up before the hoarders get here: Behavioral causes of phantom ordering in supply chains. *Journal of Operations Management*, 39, 6–22.

Sting, F. J., & Loch, C. H. (2016). Implementing operations strategy: How vertical and horizontal coordination interact. *Production and Operations Management*, 25(7), 1177–1193.

Swamidass, P. M., & Newell, W. T. (1987). Manufacturing strategy, environmental uncertainty and performance: A path analytic model. *Manage. Sci.*, 33(4), 509–524.

Swamidass, P. M., Darlow, N., & Baines, T. (2001). Evolving forms of manufacturing strategy development: evidence and implications. *International Journal of Operations & Production Management*, 21(10), 1289–1304.

Swink, M., & Way, M. (1995). Manufacturing strategy: Propositions, current research, renewed directions. *Int. J. Oper. Prod. Manage.*, 15(7), 4–26.

Tan, T. F., & Netessine, S. (2014). When does the devil make work? An empirical study of the impact of workload on worker productivity. *Management Science*, 60(6), 1574–1593.

Tennant, C., & Roberts, P. (2001). Hoshin Kanri: Implementing the catchball process. *Long Range Planning*, 34(3), 287–308.

Tsikriktsis, N. (2007). The effect of operational performance and focus on profitability: A longitudinal study of the US airline industry. *Manufacturing & Service Operations Management*, 9(4), 506–517.

Tucker, A. L., Edmondson, A. C., & Spear, S. (2002). When problem solving prevents organizational learning. *Journal of Organizational Change Management*, 15(2), 122–137.

Urda, J., & Loch, C. H. (2013). Social preferences and emotions as regulators of behavior in processes. *Journal of Operations Management*, 31(1–2), 6–23.

Voss, C. A. (1995). Alternative paradigms for manufacturing strategy. *International Journal of Operations & Production Management*, 15(4), 5–16.

Voss, C. A. (2005). Paradigms of manufacturing strategy re-visited. *International Journal of Operations & Production Management*, 25(12), 1223–1227.

Ward, P. T., & Duray, R. (2000). Manufacturing strategy in context: environment, competitive strategy and manufacturing strategy. *Journal of Operations Management*, 18(2), 123–138.

Wheelwright, S. C. (1984). Manufacturing strategy: defining the missing link. *Strategic Management Journal*, 5(1), 77–91.

Witcher, B. J., & Butterworth, R. (2001). Hoshin Kanri: Policy management in Japanese-owned UK subsidiaries. *Journal of Management Studies*, 38(5), 651–674.

Zohar, E., Mandelbaum, A., & Shimkin, N. (2002). Adaptive behavior of impatient customers in tele-queues: Theory and empirical support. *Management Science*, 48(4), 599–583.

6   Technology

Because it is an imaginary exhibit we are able to include some vast and immovable artwork, specifically the murals that cover the north and south walls of the inner courtyard at the Detroit Institute of Art. Of the 27 fresco murals that celebrated Mexican painter Diego Rivera (1886–1957) was commissioned to paint at the DIA, these two are the largest, depicting the workers at the Ford River Rouge Complex in Dearborn Michigan (Edsel Ford contributed $20,000 to the project). They provide a perfect introduction to our discussion of technology and OM. In 1927, the Ford Motor Company had begun transforming the car industry with a range of advanced technologies, including the (in)famous automated car assembly line. Further emphasizing the tumultuous nature of the times, the murals were completed between 1932 and 1933, a period that overlapped the Great Depression. This dramatic period is what Diego Rivera sought to capture in his murals. He spent three months touring Ford plants (as well as the Parke-Davis Pharmaceutical plant), preparing hundreds of sketches and concepts, in what would later become known as the Detroit Industry Murals. Rivera and his assistants worked to an intense schedule, regularly working fifteen-hour days, and completed the commission in just eight months. A large press forms a key element of the north wall mural but Rivera symbolically links this machine to the story of the Aztec goddess Coatlicue (the image is very similar to an ancient statue displayed in Mexico City's National Anthropology Museum). Rivera was illustrating how technology was increasingly central to the modern industrial world; just as in Aztec mythology Coatlicue was the mother of the gods, who gave birth to the moon, stars (and Huitzilopochtli, the god of war[1]). Throughout the mural various technologies (chemical plants, blast furnaces, foundries, conveyor belts, machine tools, etc.) are depicted, but it is the relationship between people and machines, machines imitating people and people being forced to operate like machines, that is the key theme. Of course, as Ba and Nault (2017) note, citing the steam engine and printing press as examples, it is not just physical production operations that have been shaped by 'fundamental' technological evolutions. After Gutenberg perfected the printing press in 1455, the mass production of print led to an explosion in the communication of ideas that then initiated and sustained various social and economic revolutions. Similarly, as we discussed in the introductory chapter, the steam engine (applied to mining, cotton spinning, etc.) helped initiate an industrial revolution but then the same technology applied to a service, rail transportation, began a transformation that compressed time and space and, again, instigated radical economic and social change. Although often characterized by their 'human-ness', the interaction between technology and services has also accelerated in recent years. Financial services, for example, have become "relatively intensive in their inputs of technology and/or human capital" (Field et al. 2018) with modern banks reliant upon sophisticated volume processing equipment (for the residual statements, vouchers, cash handling, etc.) and the widespread use of customer-facing, computerized technologies such as mobile apps, ATMs, telephony, etc. (Aksin et al. 2007; Xue et al. 2007). Today, even the most labour- and knowledge-intensive service operations have become increasingly technology-centric.

In this chapter, we first take an OM perspective on direct processing technologies and then turn our attention to the embodiment of technologies in new products. New Product Development (NPD) is an area where the OM/Technology nexus has received significant scholarly attention. We then shift focus to what were 'traditionally' considered to be infrastructural technologies, computerized systems like MRP and OPT. There remains an ongoing debate, the so-called productivity paradox (Polák 2017), regarding the aggregate impact of IT investment but there can be no doubt that the impacts of ever-lower cost and more ubiquitous IT have been transformational. Moreover, dramatic improvements in computing power (widely characterized by Moore's Law) underpinned the adoption of the internet with its corresponding social and economic impacts (Ba et al. 2017). In the final section therefore we reflect on the contemporary digital era, where ubiquitous infrastructure is increasingly blurring previously key OM distinctions; between production/support technology, between product and service, between customers and producers!

Direct processing technologies

As the Rivera murals vividly illustrate, the very notion of modernity is intimately linked with the appliance of scientific knowledge to production problems. Regardless of whether it is rollers flattening ingots of steel in a steel plant, injection molding to create plastic toys, or wave coating machines spreading precise amounts of chocolate over candy bars, technology defines most of the value-creating processes that are OM's central preoccupations. In addition to the transforming contributions that technology makes (i.e., power, speed, repeatability, accuracy), competitive factors have always shaped investment in operations technology. Consider, for example, how Henry Ford described the evolution of his foundry operation:

> When we cast the first "Model T" cylinders in 1910, everything in the place was done by hand; shovels and wheel-barrows abounded. The work was then either skilled or unskilled; we had moulders and we had labourers. Now we have about five percent of thoroughly skilled moulders and core setters, but the remaining 95 per cent are unskilled, or to put it more accurately, must be

skilled in exactly one operation which the most stupid man can learn within two days. The moulding is all done by machinery.

(Ford 1922, Ch. 6)

In other words, technology was central to an intent to simplify (de-skill?) the work and thus reduce wage rates, training requirements and overall costs. This is not surprising; cost reduction remains the most universal of the generic operational performance objectives[2] but, crucially, this de-skilling process did not just deliver cost benefits: it also enabled Ford's fledgling operation to hire large numbers of people (agricultural workers, etc.) without the craft skills necessary for traditional car making, thus overcoming a major capacity obstacle to high-volume production. The Ford story hints at a model of industrial competition that has been profoundly influential on how OM has traditionally framed discussions about technology, namely that firm (and market) survival is substantially affected by patterns of product and process technology co-evolution (Utterback and Abernathy 1975). Specifically, the emergence of 'dominant' (product) designs (Abernathy and Utterback 1978) creates a standardization transition such that production economies and production technologies become much more significant. Put simply, as innovative products enter fragmented markets, low and uncertain volumes will limit investment and innovation in associated (manufacturing) process technologies. Over time, as that type of product becomes established, designs that capture the (aggregate) requirements of many groups of users emerge. Competition then takes place on the basis of cost as well as product performance. Although these insights are potentially much less relevant beyond mass assembly operations (e.g., for many products, such as glass, chemicals, etc., production process innovation is central from the very beginning of the life cycle), OM research has built heavily on the idea of interdependent product-process life cycles in delineating the characteristics and benefits of different forms of technology. By profiling products according to their market volume and variety requirements (i.e., life cycle stage) it is possible to infer "appropriate" process technology. For instance, in the low-volume/high variety zone, product flows will be intermittent and workload in the various parts of the operation will vary almost every hour. The progress of work through the system could be almost anywhere and so has to be monitored and controlled. In such an operation small scale, manual, separated and flexible technology will be the norm (Yin et al. 2017). Conversely, in the high-volume/low variety zone, tasks are consistent and the volume justifies automation and scale investment. Therefore, process technology tends to be large, automated, integrated and less flexible. Critically, any design miscalculations will be extremely difficult to overcome because once the operation is committed to the capacity and nature of this structure, most subsequent changes will require further substantial capital expenditure.

New Product Development

Another area where the OM/Technology nexus has received significant scholarly attention is New Product Development (NPD). Innovative technologies transform production processes but also create new products and services (Cohen et al., 2000; Kavadias and Ulrich 2019). The POM journal in particular has been a major outlet for NPD/OM research. For example, in its first year, it published two of what would become seminal[3] articles on the topic of technology and product development (Christensen 1992a, 1992b): investigating, via a significant disk-drive industry data set, the component level implications of the technological S-curve. Interestingly, in their subsequent review of NPD in POM, Krishnan and Loch (2005) suggest that the field should "have continued the discussion on this topic"; we return to a discussion of the paucity of theory replication in OM in the final section of the book. As discussed previously, product variety creates tensions with scale economies in production, and scope economies in distribution and can lead to complex sourcing relationships (Zhou and Wan 2017). Consequently, there is enduring interest in NPD and the related drivers of product variety (e.g., Ramdas 2003). Technological architectures and, in particular, product modularity have been extensively studied given their significant implications for developing products adaptable to dynamic/future requirements (e.g., Engel et al. 2017). More generally however, and in line with the dominant process logic described in chapter 1, OM NPD research has focused on how to turn it into a more systematic process. The various stage-gate models are emblematic of this, seeking to better structure these often 'creative' and ad-hoc process so that NPD productivity (a critical competitive issue in many technology-intensive industries such as pharmaceuticals) and effectiveness are improved. The relationship between NPD and new service development (NSD) is similar to the broader manufacturing-service split; there are some excellent pieces of work (e.g., Froehle and Roth 2004; Menor and Roth 2008) and there are some significant research communities in specific topic areas, such as retail and healthcare operations, or indeed in discussing BeOM, but as an overall research theme, NSD remains something of a minority concern with OM (Hill et al. 2002). There is one really interesting aspect of NSD scholarship that is important to highlight for our subsequent discussions of digital technologies and platforms. NSD research has long recognized – albeit that much of this dialogue has taken place in adjacent fields/journals (Stevens and Dimitriadis 2004) – the need for nonlinear perspectives. Edvardsson and Olsson (1996) for example, focused on design quality and abandoned any idea of a linear/temporal model. Equally, Johnson et al. (2000) included nonlinear elements in their four-stage NSD model, emphasizing interdependence and cyclicality.

Supporting technologies: computerized control

For OM with its focus on contemporary concerns, a shifting technological context means new research challenges emerge: from an early focus on MRP, via MRPII systems to discussions of Enterprise Resource Planning (ERP) and, in the last decade, e-commerce platforms. The practical influence of many core OM methods was relatively limited until computerized production and inventory control systems were able to apply them in a rapid and efficient manner. It was while working for IBM that Joseph Orlicky and colleagues first developed what became known as Manufacturing Requirements Planning (MRP). MRP uses the product

Bill of Material as the basis for planning given that the demand for most components is actually a function of demand for the final product. Over time this evolved into Manufacturing Resource Planning (i.e., MRP II) as it integrated decision criteria from other functional areas (sales, staffing, etc.). There are many fascinating parallels with contemporary discussions of digital technology in the MRP 'story'. As detailed in Mabert (2007) the American Production and Inventory Control Society (APICS) – in collaboration with IBM – was an early champion of MRP. The 'Big Blue' sending its 'MRP Mafia' on the road to local APICS meetings and running MRP Workshops at Annual and Regional Meetings of the (then) American Institute for Decision Sciences (today the Decision Sciences Institute, DSI). At the time MRP was seen (or at least promoted) as nothing short of revolutionary, indeed Joseph Orlicky (frequently) gave a lecture titled "The Copernican Revolution[4] in Production and Inventory Control". One interesting side note to this evolution was the development of scheduling software product OPT (Optimized Production Timetables, later Technologies). Based on the work of Eliyahu Goldratt this software, essentially a variation of MRP which combines the bill of materials with a routing file that can identify and prioritize (using a "secret" algorithm) all parts movement through bottlenecks, had significant impact. Watson et al. (2007) reported that – at that time – more than 100 companies worldwide had purchased OPT, at a minimum price of $2 million.[5]

From MRP to Enterprise Resource Planning (ERP)

ERP, a logical extension of MRP, was designed to offer, in theory at least, real-time resource accountability across all business units and facilities (Jacobs and Bendoly 2003). Although appealing – the global enterprise system market was worth more than $400 billion US dollars in 2018 – especially for senior (finance) managers, the complexity of any large-scale organization means that significant implementation issues nearly always arise. In fact, for many years the introduction of ERP systems has been one of the most common organizational change events (Herold et al. 2007). For some firms, ERP has been a way to integrate information and processes across organizational functions, increasing efficiency and effectiveness and leading to improvements in firm performance. Unfortunately, there have also been many high-profile failures[6]. Indeed, for many (the majority?) firms exploiting promised capability proved to be a secondary concern, ultimately lagging far behind simply "getting the system to run". A significant part of ERP research follows this 'implementation turn', repeatedly observing that ERP adoption is risky, and highlighting (unsurprising) insights such as the importance of investing in change management (e.g., Morris and Venkatesh 2010) and support structures like training, online support and help desks.

The ERP phenomenon has further evolved with subsequent technological shifts; moving from 'on-premises' software to on-demand software solutions such as application service provision (ASP) and, most recently, software-as-a-service (SaaS). SaaS, defined as an application or service that is deployed across a network, provide ERP access on a recurring fee basis, where users typically rent the applications/services from a central provider. Although studies of SaaS ERP systems are rare they appear to have significant cost and implementation advantages.[7] This shift brings other emerging issues for OM research to the fore. In such systems, (company and customer) data is often located outside local firewalls, hardware is owned by third parties and yet firms remain responsible for controls and regulatory compliance. This further blurs the boundaries between core operational functions and purchasing/supply chain management. The Behavioral OM lens is also relevant. When technology is changing people are exposed to risk and uncertainty and, especially with platform/infrastructural technologies, the influence of bias, heuristics, preferences and norms will inevitably feature. From senior management confirmation bias (and overconfidence and framing/anchoring, etc.) limiting the motivation for genuine technological experimentation, to the absence of a psychologically safe culture to underpin group performance. Standardized project management approaches, like stage-gate models, can even act to make things worse by hiding "behavioural" issues (Loch 2017).

Digital technologies

The changes occurring to ERP systems are just one manifestation of the distributed digital technologies that have altered the operating models of many industries. In service operations like banking, for example, the result of asynchronous client interactions, opportunities for better marketing/operations alignment, enhanced knowledge dissemination, etc. have driven down costs, and 'on-line' systems appeal to customers because they can be more cost and time efficient – for instance, by combining access to/modification of information from multiple sources – and this helps improve customer satisfaction. Another digital technology with (potentially) revolutionary implications for OM is 3D printing or Direct Digital Manufacturing (DDM). Some have suggested that DDM will eventually replace all traditional tool-based manufacturing[8] (D'Aveni 2015) noting how, when integrated with advanced design and modelling software it should be possible to optimize designs resulting in, for example, reduced weight and reduced assembly by integrating functionality of parts (Chen et al. 2015). To date, the economic case is far from clear (Baumers and Holweg 2019) with DDM's higher costs meaning it is mainly used for tasks, such as prototyping, 'soft tooling', and on-demand creation of customized and spare parts (Khajavi et al. 2015), in support of tool-based manufacturing. That said, even if DDM fails to displace volume manufacturing in the near future, it is likely to shape core OM considerations (e.g., routing and scheduling) for low-volume manufacturing. Of course, a truly widespread adoption of DDM would drive fundamental structural changes to established business models (Holmström and Partanen 2014). Perhaps digital product information (Främling et al. 2007) will increasingly replace inventory as the focus of OSCM and manufacturing will become a resource that lies outside most firm's boundaries, directly comparable to the SaaS evolution of ERP described earlier. Consider the widespread adoption of radio frequency identification devices (RFID[9]). This is not a new technology[10] and its adoption, driven over the last 20 years by various powerful organizations, including the US DoD and large retailers like Wal-Mart, Tesco and Metro, is still far from ubiquitous. That said, the 2018 global market, approximately 16.5 billion tags, was worth more than $11.0 billion and RFID is increasingly seen as a key component of manufacturing (Ferrer et al. 2011; Chongwatpol and Sharda 2013, etc.), supply chain management (Sarac et al. 2010) and the so-called "internet of things" (Da Xu et al. 2014).

The final part of our short review of digital technologies turns to the recent improvements in AI, especially machine learning (ML). Here again we are witnessing the leverage of exponential growth in data and data processing but with consequences that have profound implications for OM. Historically, programmes were created by meticulous process work, programmers carefully mapping inputs to outputs, but machine-learning systems use categories of general algorithms to establish such mappings 'independently', typically via access to extremely large data sets. ML methods have made impressive gains in perception and cognition, increasingly emulating essential aspects of human work.[11] These systems have the potential to further transform the socio-techno-economic landscape, creating new opportunities for business value creation and cost reduction. However undoubtedly beneficial/disruptive these technologies[12] are, studying infrastructures/platforms, rather than technological tools – like Rivera's Press – with a fixed and measurable output, represents an emerging ontological challenge for OM. Such technologies have direct and indirect effects on productivity, through the absolute quantity of labour necessary, relative levels of non-IT capital (e.g., cloud manufacturing) and impact on the intermediate inputs (e.g., inventory control, energy efficiency, etc.) needed to produce a given level of output. Cheng and Nault (2007) for example, examined the effect of upstream (i.e., the reverse direction to flows of goods) IT investment and found 'spillover' effects that, via improved co-ordination and control, increased focal firm productivity (an effect they later (2012) show was magnified by higher levels of industry concentration).

At the same time, for all the promise, their real impact is still the subject of substantial debate with labour productivity growth rates in many developed economies low since the mid-2000s and little sign of impact on aggregate productivity statistics. Brynjolfsson et al. (2017) present some potential explanations (including technology being over-hyped and mis-measured) for this 'missing productivity'. For instance, perhaps new technology benefits are only being enjoyed by a relatively small fraction of the economy? There is evidence that differences in productivity (and market shares, profit margins, wages) between frontier and average firms in the same industry have increased.

Concluding comments

One explanation for the missing digital productivity has particularly striking implications for OM scholarship and practice. It asserts that while there is good reason to be optimistic about the future productivity growth potential of new technologies, it still takes a considerable time to be able to sufficiently harness new technologies. Compare this with the earlier discussion of the impact of DDM? Up to this point, we have been presenting an essentially passive narrative driven by the 'evolution' of technology, whereby OM with its process logic is essentially agnostic in the face of technological novelty. Yet if OM only ever studies new technologies, they will, axiomatically, be exploring nascent applications and any findings will tend to be, as with ERP research, dominated by early stage challenges. Some scholars have looked beyond this initial phase. Bendoly (2001) for example, drew a prescient distinction between the ERP "concept" and ERP "systems", arguing that ERP "systems" should be looked at as an infrastructure designed to support the capability of all other tools and processes and, as such, benefits could only be properly understood when such systems are fully established. Likewise, it isn't until sufficient stock of a new technology is built (plus the necessary complementary processes and assets) that it will be visible in industry-level economic data. Ironically, the more profound and far-reaching the potential restructuring, the longer the time lag may be between the initial invention of the technology and its full impact on the economy and society.

These new competitive battlegrounds, these platforms (McIntyre and Srinivasan 2017; Van Alstyne et al. 2016, etc.) are also creating new (operating) strategies. Using an RBV logic, the scarce, valuable and (hopefully) inimitable assets are the community and the resources (i.e., Uber and cars, AirBNB and rooms, etc.) ideas and information the members of the community own and contribute. Equally, given that platforms create value by facilitating interactions, the dominant OM process logic, whereby activity chains are optimized, becomes less important than questions of connectivity and governance.

In short, digital technology is asking some potentially existential questions of OM; researchers will have to provide clearer definitions of the phenomena and accept that it that may necessitate consideration of a very different units of analysis.

Notes

1 The mural also depict scientists producing medical vaccines and poison gas.
2 Although it is important to note how, in 2019, the 'alternative' economic models of many high-profile, high-tech operations are driving very different investment profiles.
3 These articles, despite relatively modest citation levels (cf. his later book), have a legitimate claim to be the most impactful OM research ever. Christensen's terms, "innovator's dilemma" and "disruptive/architectural innovation", have entered the global business lexicon and changed the way we think about innovation in both practice and theory. As Krishnan and Loch (2005) note, few other OM authors have appeared on the cover of *Forbes* magazine!
4 This lecture included critical comments about EOQ, etc. comparing it with views on the solar system before Copernicus introduced the idea that the planets orbit the sun.
5 It has also been subject to many commercial challenges. As Watson et al. (2007) report, M&M Mars Company sued the firm following a failed implementation and sought the release of the OPT algorithms in an effort to prove that OPT was actually an inappropriate solution for their specific situation and could not have deliver the promised benefits. This matter was settled; however, the lawsuit combined with Goldratt's departure shortly thereafter, to concentrate on management education and concept development, tarnished TOC in the eyes of many.

6 Some have estimated failure rates to be greater than 60% (Devadoss and Pan 2007).

7 Challenges remain, of course: latency and network/scalable storage limits, integrity of the provider, alternative arrangements during service disruptions, poor interconnectivity and interfacing with other existing applications, etc.

8 In the same way as direct printing is incrementally replacing offset printing in the typographic industry.

9 Unlike barcodes, RFID tags do not need a direct line of sight to a reader, meaning it can be easier/quicker to use and tags can be embedded in an object. There are two basic types of RFID. Passive tags collect energy from a nearby RFID reader whereas active tags have a local power source and can be detected at a significant distance from the reader.

10 The term RFID first appeared in a patent granted in 1983 but the technology has clear antecedents in many areas, including the work of Soviet scientist Léon Theremin, who developed a passive listening device activated by EM waves from an outside source and the transponders routinely used since WWII to identify aircraft as friend or foe. Today the technology is used in a wide variety of operational applications: in contactless transit, access and payment applications; in the tagging of domestic and commercial animals, driven by legal requirements in many more territories, with 540 million tags being used for this sector in 2018.

11 Using any real examples in a rapidly changing technological landscape means that they will inevitably be dated by the time you read this footnote – sorry – but, as an illustration a neural network system recently matched the skin cancer diagnosis performance of 21 board-certified dermatologists (Esteva et al. 2017). Brynjolfsson et al. (2017) highlight other examples; reporting how error rates in a 2017 ImageNet[11] photo labelling competition has fallen to 2.2%, from over 30% in 2010. Similarly, they detail how voice recognition error rates have decreased to 5.5% from 8.5% over the past year. The 5% threshold being broadly equivalent to human performance.

12 A platform may include physical components, tools and rules to facilitate development, a collection of technical standards to support interoperability, or any combination of these things. Serving as a stable nexus or foundation, a platform can organize the technical development of interchangeable, complementary components and permit them to interact with one another. Boudreau (2010).

References

Abernathy, W. J., & Utterback, J. M. (1978). Patterns of industrial innovation. *Technology Review*, 80(7), 40–47.

Aksin, Z., Armony, M., & Mehrotra, V. (2007). The modern call center: A multi-disciplinary perspective on operations management research. *Production and Operations Management*, 16(6), 665–688.

Ba, S., & Nault, B. R. (2017). Emergent themes in the interface between economics of information systems and management of technology. *Production and Operations Management*, 26(4), 652–666.

Baumers, M., Beltrametti, L., Gasparre, A., & Hague, R. (2017). Informing additive manufacturing technology adoption: Total cost and the impact of capacity utilisation. *International Journal of Production Research*, 1–14.

Baumers, M., & Holweg, M. (2019). On the economics of additive manufacturing: Experimental findings. *Journal of Operations Management*, In Press.

Bendoly, E. (2001). ERP systems and supply chain technologies: a caveat for B2B e-procurement. FedEx White Paper Series, *Whitepaper*, 28–36.

Boudreau, K. (2010). Open platform strategies and innovation: Granting access vs. devolving control. *Management Science*, 56(10), 1849–1872.

Brem, A., Nylund, P. A., & Schuster, G. (2016). Innovation and de facto standardization: The influence of dominant design on innovative performance, radical innovation, and process innovation. *Technovation*, 50, 79–88.

Brynjolfsson, E., Rock, D., & Syverson, C. (2017). *Artificial intelligence and the modern productivity paradox: A clash of expectations and statistics* (No. w24001). National Bureau of Economic Research.

Chen, D., Heyer, S., Ibbotson, S., Salonitis, K., Steingrímsson, J. G., & Thiede, S. (2015). Direct digital manufacturing: definition, evolution, and sustainability implications. *Journal of Cleaner Production*, 107, 615–625.

Cheng, Z., & Nault, B. R. (2007). Industry level supplier-driven IT spillovers. *Management Science*, 53(8), 119–1216.

Choi, K., Narasimhan, R., & Kim, S. W. (2016). Opening the technological innovation black box: The case of the electronics industry in Korea. *European Journal of Operational Research*, 250(1), 192–203.

Chongwatpol, J., & Sharda, R. (2013). RFID-enabled track and traceability in job-shop scheduling environment. *European Journal of Operational Research*, 227(3), 453–463.

Christensen, C. M. (1992a). Exploring the limits of the technology S-curve, Part I: Component technologies. *Production and Operations Management*, 1(4), 334–357.

Christensen, C. M. (1992b) Exploring the limits of the technology S-curve, Part II: Architectural technologies. *Production and Operations Management*, 1(4), 358–366.

Cohen, M. A., Eliashberg, J., & Ho, T. H. (2000). An analysis of several new product performance metrics. *Manufacturing & Service Operations Management*, 2(4), 337–349.

D'Aveni, R. (2015). The 3-D printing revolution. *Harvard Business Review*, 93(5), 40–48.

Da Xu, L., He, W., & Li, S. (2014). Internet of things in industries: A survey. *IEEE Transactions on Industrial Informatics*, 10(4), 2233–2243.

Despeisse, M., Baumers, M., Brown, P., Charnley, F., Ford, S. J., Garmulewicz, A., Knowles, S., Minshall, T. H. W., Mortara, L., Reed-Tsochas, F. P., & Rowley, J. (2017). Unlocking value for a circular economy through 3D printing: A research agenda. *Technological Forecasting and Social Change*, 115, 75–84.

Devadoss, P., & Pan, S. L. (2007). Enterprise systems use: Towards a structurational analysis of enterprise systems induced organizational transformation. *Communications of the Association for Information Systems*, 19(1), 17.

Edvardsson, B., & Olsson, J. (1996). Key concepts for new service development. *Service Industries Journal*, 16(2), 140–164.

Engel, A., Browning, T. R., & Reich, Y. (2017). Designing products for adaptability: Insights from four industrial cases. *Decision Sciences*, 48(5), 875–917.

Esteva, A., Kuprel, B., Novoa, R. A., Ko, J., Swetter, S. M., Blau, H. M., & Thrun, S. (2017). Dermatologist-level classification of skin cancer with deep neural networks. *Nature*, 542(7639), 115–118.

Ferrer, G., Heath, S. K., & Dew, N. (2011). An RFID application in large job shop remanufacturing operations. *International Journal of Production Economics*, 133(2), 612–621.

Field, J. M., Victorino, L., Buell, R. W., Dixon, M. J., Meyer Goldstein, S., Menor, L. J., . . . & Zhang, J. J. (2018). Service operations: what's next?. *Journal of Service Management*, 29(1), 55–97.

Ford, H. (1922). *My Life and Work, in collaboration with S. Crowther*. London: William.

Framling, K., Ala-Risku, T., Karkkainen, M., & Holmstrom, J. (2007). Design patterns for managing product life cycle information. *Communications of the ACM*, 50(6), 75–79.

Froehle, C. M., & Roth, A. V. (2004). New measurement scales for evaluating perceptions of the technology-mediated customer service experience. *Journal of Operations Management*, 22(1), 1–21.

Gaimon, C., Hora, M., & Ramachandran, K. (2017). Towards building multidisciplinary knowledge on management of technology: An introduction to the special issue. *Production and Operations Management*, 26(4), 567–578.

Gattiker, T. F., & Goodhue, D. L. (2005). What happens after ERP implementation: Understanding the impact of interdependence and differentiation on plant-level outcomes. *MIS Quarterly*, 559–585.

Herold, D. M., Fedor, D. B., & Caldwell, S. D. (2007). Beyond change management: A multilevel investigation of contextual and personal influences on employees' commitment to change. *Journal of Applied Psychology*, 92(4), 942.

Hill, A. V., Collier, D. A., Froehle, C. M., Goodale, J. C., Metters, R. D., & Verma, R. (2002). Research opportunities in service process design. *Journal of Operations Management*, 20(2), 189–202.

Holmström, J., & Partanen, J. (2014). Digital manufacturing-driven transformations of service supply chains for complex products. Supply Chain Management: *An International Journal*, 19(4), 421–430.

Holmström, J., Holweg, M., Khajavi, S. H., & Partanen, J. (2016). The direct digital manufacturing (r)evolution: Definition of a research agenda. *Operations Management Research*, 9(1–2), 1–10.

Jacobs, F. R., & Bendoly, E. (2003). Enterprise resource planning: Developments and directions for operations management research. *European Journal of Operational Research*, 146(2), 233–240.

Johnson, S.P., Menor, L.J., Roth, A.V., Chase, R.B., (2000). A critical evaluation of the new service development process: integrating service innovation and service design. In: Fitzsimmons, J.A., Fitzsimmons, M.J. (Eds.), *New Service Development—Creating Memorable Experiences*. Sage Publications, Thousand Oaks, CA, pp. 1–32.

Khajavi, S. H., Partanen, J., Holmström, J., & Tuomi, J. (2015). Risk reduction in new product launch: A hybrid approach combining direct digital and tool-based manufacturing. *Computers in Industry*, 74, 29–42.

Krishnan, V., & Loch, C. H. (2005). A retrospective look at production and operations management articles on new product development. *Production and Operations Management*, 14(4), 433–441.

Kavadias, S. & Ulrich, K.T. (2019). *Innovation and New Product Development: Reflections and Insights from the Research Published in the First 20 Years of M&SOM*, SSRN Electronic Journal, 10.2139/ssrn.3385783.

Loch, C. H. (2017). Creativity and risk taking aren't rational: Behavioral operations in MOT. *Production and Operations Management*, 26(4), 591–604.

Mabert, V. A. (2007). The early road to material requirements planning. *Journal of Operations Management*, 25(2), 346–356.

Mabert, V. A., Soni, A., & Venkataramanan, M. A. (2003). Enterprise resource planning: Managing the implementation process. *European Journal of Operational Research*, 146(2), 302–314.

McIntyre, D. P., & Srinivasan, A. (2017). Networks, platforms, and strategy: Emerging views and next steps. *Strategic Management Journal*, 38(1), 141–160.

Menor, L. J., & Roth, A. V. (2008). New service development competence and performance: An empirical investigation in retail banking. *Production and Operations Management*, 17(3), 267–284.

Moehrle, M. G., Wustmans, M., & Gerken, J. M. (2018). How business methods accompany technological innovations: A case study using semantic patent analysis and a novel informetric measure. *R&D Management*, 48(3), 331–342.

Muhanna, A., Waleed, M., & Stoel, D. (2010). How do investors value IT? An empirical investigation of the value relevance of IT capability and IT spending across industries. *Journal of Information Systems*, 24, 43–66.

Murray, C. C., & Chu, A. G. (2015). The flying sidekick traveling salesman problem: Optimization of drone-assisted parcel delivery. *Transport. Res. Part C: Emerg. Technol.*, 54, 86–109.

Ngai, E. W. T., Moon, K. K. L., Riggins, F. J., & Candace, Y. Y. (2008). RFID research: An academic literature review (1995–2005) and future research directions. *International Journal of Production Economics*, 112(2), 510–520.

Polák, P. (2017). The productivity paradox: A meta-analysis. *Information Economics and Policy*, 38, 38–54.

Ramdas, K. (2003). Managing product variety: An integrative review and research directions. *Production and Operations Management*, 12(1), 79–101.

Remus, D., & Levy, F. (2017). Can robots be lawyers: Computers, lawyers, and the practice of law. *Geo. J. Legal Ethics*, 30, 501.

Sarac, A., Absi, N., & Dauzère-Pérès, S. (2010). A literature review on the impact of RFID technologies on supply chain management. *International Journal of Production Economics*, 128(1), 77–95.

Shalley, C. E., & Gilson, L. L. (2017). Creativity and the management of technology: Balancing creativity and standardization. *Production and Operations Management*, 26(4), 605–616.

Stevens, E., & Dimitriadis, S. (2004). New service development through the lens of organisational learning: Evidence from longitudinal case studies. *Journal of Business Research*, 57(10), 1074–1084.

Sykes, T.-A. (2015). Support structures and their impacts on employee outcomes: A longitudinal field study of an enterprise system implementation. *MIS Quarterly*, 39(2).

Utterback, J. M., & Abernathy, W. J. (1975). A dynamic model of process and product innovation. *Omega*, 3(6), 639–656.

Van Alstyne, M. W., Parker, G. G., & Choudary, S. P. (2016). Pipelines, platforms, and the new rules of strategy. *Harvard Business Review*, 94(4), 54–62.

Morris, M. G., & Venkatesh, V. (2010). Job characteristics and job satisfaction: understanding the role of enterprise resource planning system implementation. *MIS Quarterly*, 34(1).

Watson, K. J., Blackstone, J. H., & Gardiner, S. C. (2007). The evolution of a management philosophy: The theory of constraints. *Journal of Operations Management*, 25(2), 387–402.

Xue, M., Hitt, L. M., & Harker, P. T. (2007). Customer efficiency, channel usage, and firm performance in retail banking. *Manufacturing & Service Operations Management*, 9(4), 535–558.

Yin, Y., Stecke, K. E., Swink, M., & Kaku, I. (2017). Lessons from seru production on manufacturing competitively in a high cost environment. *Journal of Operations Management*, 49, 67–76.

Zhou, Y. M., & Wan, X. (2017). Product variety, sourcing complexity, and the bottleneck of coordination. *Strategic Management Journal*, 38(8), 1569–1587.

7 The future

OM *Gesamtkunstwerk* or just more collage?

The final room in our imaginary gallery contains an amazing piece of Georgian architecture and a collage, embracing different perspectives on the idea of artistic synthesis that help inform these final integrative reflections. The first is Pulteney Bridge across the River Avon in Bath,[1] England. Completed in 1774, it is over 20 metres long and is unusual in having shops built across its full span on both sides. Scottish Architect Robert Adam designed Pulteney Bridge in a Palladian style[2] – in an echo of our earlier discussion of the Venice Arsenale – but, critically, he was also was an advocate of a form of harmonizing or integrating synthesis, whereby the architect is responsible for the design of the total (interior and exterior) of a building. Although there is some OM *Gesamtkunstwerk* ("total artwork"), where distinct universal theories and perspectives have been proposed (e.g., Schmenner and Swink 1998; Sampson and Froehle 2006) this has not been a priority for OM scholarship. The accompanying collage is by Eduardo Paolozzi,[3] *Lessons of Last Time* (1947), from his *Bunk* series of works. It combines many overlapping images; clipped newspapers reports of Sigmund Freud boarding an airplane, a story about Albert Einstein enquiring about an aircraft altimeter and discussing the meaning of time, magazine adverts and storage instructions for industrial pumps. A child of the interwar years, collage held real significance for Paolozzi who had grown up in a society in which nothing was left to waste. He also came to realize that many adverts, for say food and cars, spoke more eloquently and economically of dreams than conventional art. OM is full of such collage and is, in many ways, the archetype 'mash up' discipline.[4] Meredith and Pilkington (2018) used citation analyses of the three oldest OM journals over three decades in comparison to 27 Management, Operations Research/Management Science (OR/MS), Marketing, Practice and Engineering journals and confirmed that OM "cites these journals about twenty-five times more often than they cite our journals". Much of this book has detailed how the field appropriates insights and analytical constructs from various adjacent theoretical and empirical specialisms but there are also other less mainstream 'borrows'. For example, systems dynamics (SD) approaches, originally derived from electro-mechanical design, have been used to study various operational challenges.[5] Equally, Perrow's (2011) Normal Accident Theory (which holds that no matter what organizations do, accidents are inevitable in complex, tightly – coupled systems) has been used in various OM (and SCM) studies. Wolf (2001) applied the theory to petrochemical plants and refinery accidents, confirming the relevance of the lens but also noting that many approaches to operational efficiency can actually increase the risk of normal accidents. Does such eclecticism matter? Should the OM discipline develop more of its own theories and, if not, what are the new collages to be shaped?

OM *Gesamtkunstwerk?*

In first asking whether OM should develop more of its own theory, reflections regarding the 'proper' role for theory are instructive (cf. Schmenner and Swink 1998; Schmenner et al. 2009; Boer et al. 2015). Phenomena should be clearly defined, preferably with unambiguous measures so that a theory can tell a story that explains why laws work as they do and how, in which ways and subject to which limitations. Wacker (2004) argues that good formal conceptual definitions are *necessary* conditions for construct validity (content validity, criterion validity, convergent validity and discriminant validity). Given this, it is intriguing to reflect that few OM 'theories' have been used/tested more than once (Kenworthy and Balakrishnan 2016). Does this imply poor theory development or perhaps an instinctive default to the greater legitimacy of work from, often larger, communities of scholarship? Frohlich and Dixon (2006), recognizing that OM replication studies were rare, edited the first (and, to date, only?) special issue (SI) focused on this. Their editorial, which has only been cited 23 times in the intervening 12 years, is framed with a clear affirmation that strong theory and insight can only come from continual testing of theory via replication, Kuhn's (1962) "normal science", and a recognition that "[e]very academic discipline needs a healthy balance between the publication of novel results and replicated studies". Set against this laudable objective, their observations from the SI process contain numerous insights for this debate. They only received what they called the "somewhat modest tally" of 25 submissions and concluded that OM researchers were reluctant to revisit other's work (all the replications were of concepts that were 10+ years old). Moreover, reviewers were also uncomfortable with replication studies, as one potential reviewer replied, "I can't waste my time looking at something that is already published". Ironically, those who did review for the SI found it interesting and enjoyable and when the editors reached out to the scholars whose studies were being replicated they were all "flattered that something that they had published years ago was [being] studied anew". In conclusion they asked what remains to be replicated and despite answering "virtually everything" they questioned if the OM discipline was up to the challenge, observing (we can now say accurately) that, if replications didn't become more popular in the next 10 years, an entire generation (early 1980s–2010s) of OM output would have been "mostly one-off studies and unsubstantiated conclusions".

A related argument for increased homegrown theorizing, or at least limiting the use of adjacent constructs, might be found when formally questioning their actual utility. Kenworthy and Balakrishnan (2016) for example developed a "screening model" built on a series of necessary conditions for imported theory to be value adding. They apply this model in a critical appraisal of the use of RBV in OM (Schroeder et al. 2002). Their first condition is that it must be relevant to OM and its central concerns (i.e., processes, services, etc.), and here they note both the potential disadvantage of different units of analysis (OM's functional versus RBV's firm-level) and the Bromiley and Rau (2016) argument that "operations activities per se do not tie to sustained competitive advantage". Their second condition is that the theory must offer strong prediction and explanation, grounded in rigorous testing within its own discipline and needing *minimal* adjustment on importation (e.g., of variables and/or relationships amongst variables). Here, they note that the predictive power of RBV has been regularly challenged, with many highlighting its potentially tautological characteristics, and observe that there has been a great deal of ad-hoc adjustment, not the least in terms of resource specificity.[6] Ultimately, they offer the damning verdict that it "does not appear that OM is particularly well-served by employing RBV for scientific knowledge creation".

Another motivation for novel synthesis may emerge from concerns that OM, avowedly a pragmatic field, increasingly seems disconnected from practice? This concern was described in the introductory chapter, under the heading 'Where's the Management?' but continues today. When launching the Journal of Operations Management design science department, the departmental editors explained how they saw design science research (DSR) as a strategy, aimed at using knowledge to design and implement actions, processes or systems to achieve desired outcomes in practice (cf. Holmström et al. 2009). For the editors, DSR involves deep engagement with real-life OM problems or opportunities, taking 'products' from the "high ground of theory" to be used in the ever-changing, under-determined and insecure "swamp of practice" (terms coined by Schon 1983). Yet the extent to which novel OM theory is needed because as a community we are interested in researching and supporting the "changed realities" faced by firms is contested. There are some, like Narasimhan (2014) who argue for scholarship that enhances knowledge *and* advances practice but it is important to reflect on Ketokivi's honest commentary (Schmenner et al. 2009):

> Theories are . . . perhaps the most important instrument through which researchers come to understand one another's arguments. Whether theories also help us understand real-life phenomena – that is an entirely different question. To be sure, it is highly unlikely that theories formulated by academics automatically coincide with managerial interests. Most of us are literature-driven not problem-driven in our research.
>
> (p. 342)

One result of being 'literature-driven' and being incentivized primarily by journal output performance can be too much propositional "boxes-and-arrows" work (Delbridge and Fiss 2013); what Schmenner (in Schmenner et al. 2009) calls the *archetype* theory-building approach:

The hypotheses to be tested allegedly derive from theory. The hypotheses are not merely guesses but predictions from one or another social science theory. A great literature search has been accomplished to isolate these hypotheses and to defend them" but then "the empirical results are often mixed. Some of the hypotheses are supported but others are not. The lack of support for the theory standing behind these hypotheses, and for which so much searching in the literature was done, does not lead to any criticism of the theory nor any claim that it has been overturned by the empirical results.

(p. 340)

More methods, more rigour . . .

In the absence of (or even much of a search for) distinct, cumulatively tested OM theory, most researchers are motivated by empirical work. Traditionally this engagement with practice involved an eclectic variety of methods to collect and analyse data but contemporary scholarship is dominated by ever more sophisticated statistical modelling. For example, noting the earlier discussion regarding theory building, the application of mediation perspectives has proved particularly popular. In the last decade, however, several of the key assumptions underlying such statistical reasoning have been challenged, with explicit suggestions that too much OM work is built on untrustworthy statistical inference. Some of this critique comes from diffusion lag between the OM community and developments in the wider methodological literature (especially complex mediation[7] models such as the ones that involve multimediator and moderated mediation). The Malhotra et al. (2014) study for example, highlights common inadequacies in OM mediation studies and recommends convenient ways to improve them. Similarly, there has been increased focus on what is, in the econometrics literature, labelled the problem of endogeneity. There are legitimate concerns regarding the sources of variance of exogenous variables and potential tests for them (Guide and Ketokivi 2015) and while they can likely never be fully eliminated, consideration of theoretical and logical simultaneity (reverse causality), avoiding Common Method Bias (when measures for independent and dependent variables are collected from the same rating source) and various robustness checks to rule out the likelihood of omitted variables can all help.

To rehearse many of these debates in detail is beyond the scope of this book (and patience of the author!) but to note, important technical improvements have been made to the execution and analysis of fieldwork, that have significant implications – especially if more macro-micro studies, more theory building, etc. is to be attempted. However, we should be vigilant to the risks raised by Schmenner and Swink (1998) when they quote Kaplan (1964) and his assertion that behavioural science often has an unhealthy fixation on methodology:

There are behavioral scientists who, in their desperate search for scientific status, give the impression that they don't much care what they do if only they do it right: substance gives way to form. And here a vicious circle is engendered; when the outcome is seen to be empty, this is taken as pointing all the more to the need for a better methodology.

(p. 406)

In other words, even if it remains a net importer of theory, OM must not forget that all conceptual and empirical research is framed by theoretical paradigm and method and also by ontology and epistemology and by subjectivist, positivist, realist orientations. Ontology and epistemology are undoubtedly contested notions but critical nonetheless as researchers, regardless of their awareness of their position, cannot simply change these like they might change an item of clothing. Obviously, most OM adopts and will continue to adopt an objectivist/positivistic view, such that key aspects of phenomena being studied can be revealed by objective, quantitative data. Yet, however much a minority interest they may be in OM, subjectivist views are also invaluable. Engaging with contextually embedded, multiple representations of reality raises possibilities for rich understanding and potentially the foundations for further research. Consider the opportunities afforded by alternative interpretations, even when discussing something as apparently axiomatic as the basic definition of OM. Lovejoy (1998, p. 106) suggests that, "OM is the selection and management of transformation processes that create value for society". OM takes these ideas (value, waste, etc.) for granted whereas other fields, like economic sociology, anthropology and marketing have a long tradition of discussing their subjective nature (e.g., Corvellec and Hultman 2014). For these fields, definitions of value are conditioned and embedded in the cultural characteristics and symbolic systems that, in any given context, define what is important, meaningful, desirable, or worthwhile. As an exemplar, Styhre's (2001) work is fascinating. In studying the notion of kaizen in Sweden, the author undertakes three major separations: separating it temporally from scientific management, culturally from Japanese companies and Japanese workers, and, finally, from the collective to the level of the individual.[8] Kaizen in this analysis is thus no longer "a Japanese, Taylorist, collective practice, but instead a Swedish, non-Taylorist, individual-oriented management technique" (p. 804).

The future?

Several scholars have proposed ways forward. Schmenner (in Schmenner et al, 2009) argued, perhaps counter-intuitively, for good empirical work that is *independent* of theory and not overly pre-occupied with method. This approach is echoed by Narasimhan (2014) who reflects that one common characteristic of the seminal ideas that have shaped OM is that they relied on observational studies and conceptual reasoning. He goes on to conclude that a greater emphasis on qualitative research (cf. MacCarthy et al. 2013) might be the basis for an "intellectual renewal" and help extend the frontiers of a mature discipline. The Lusch commentary on Schmenner (in Schmenner et al. 2009, p. 343) similarly proposes that "a reassessment of the dominant logic of operations management would be fruitful" before (unsurprisingly) proffering the tenets of the Service-Dominant (SD) logic as a potentially useful way forward.[9] These notions of disciplinary reshaping (however naïve they may be given current scholarly incentive structures) seem particularly important if OM is to do a better job of developing robust insight into the non-manufacturing world. Ketokivi et al. (2017) propose a potentially important contribution to this question of effective theory development, albeit not explicitly aimed at the OM community. They focus on how important metaphor/analogy (e.g., flow, nexus of contracts, information processing) are in both helping *ex-post* presentation of theory and *ex-ante* theoretical reasoning. To avoid "the risk of introducing a constant stream of novel ideas without adequate evaluation", they adapt Toulmin's general model for describing argument[10] (2003) and introduce structured questions to guide the evaluation of reasoning by analogy (relevance, structural soundness and factual validity). Critically, they also emphasize Toulmin's observation that the purpose of theorizing is to convince a wider audience.

New OM collages?

One of the wonderful aspects of the idea of OM as a series of conceptual collages is the almost infinite number of future options it creates. In this section we will illustrate this by exploring two such options but the process of crafting a collage, overlaying different layers of various materials to build something new, also highlights a way of building new OM insight by developing conceptualizations at more than one level of analysis that "are likely to yield theories with a broad domain of applicability" (Narasimhan 2014). Just as the introductory chapter stresses how locating the OM story too narrowly in the (UK) industrial revolution misses the intrinsically human characteristics (i.e., division of labour, specialization, etc.) of many of the principles later reified by scholars; such a-contextual thinking also misses earlier European industrial practice and, much earlier, Chinese innovations, such as the flexible production systems creating the Terracotta Army. Moreover, it matters that the Industrial Revolution, centred on the transformation of the UK textile industry, was stimulated as much by a rapidly growing empire centred around India and enforced by UK Naval power as it was by technical and systems innovations. Equally, it is important to understand (e.g., when determining a best practice) that the mid-19th-century introduction of interchangeable parts, a key part of the 'America system of manufacturing' that allowed manufacturers to break fundamentally with the craft model of production and fully exploit the division of labour, came to the fore in a country unhindered by long-established forms of organizational "focus" embodied in structures such as craft guilds and supported by the growth of a nationwide distribution and communications network (i.e., the railroad), allowing easier moves towards more vertically integrated, and larger scale, modes of production. More recently, during the middle-1980s, macroeconomic volatility was substantially reduced; a phenomenon now known as the "great moderation",[11] and it has been argued that the greater predictability in economic and financial performance associated with this period caused firms to hold less capital and to be less concerned about liquidity positions – factors with a potentially profound impact on OM policies. Similarly, outsourcing decisions and subsequent supply chain and OM challenges, as well as inflationary pressures and credit policies were profoundly shaped by the emergence of China as a global economic actor, entering the WTO, etc. There is a body of work which connects OM practices with, say, measures[12] of environmental uncertainty, complexity and dynamism (e.g., Ward et al. 1995; Azadegan et al. 2013), but Hausman et al. (2013) is one of the few papers to take an explicitly *macro-micro* perspective, using a World Bank data set to explore the impact of logistics performance (time, cost and reliability) on (increased volume of) global bilateral trade. Interestingly, it is where more specific, objective contextual factors are studied, such as with Shah and Ward's (2003) investigation of the effect of plant size, plant age and unionization status on the likelihood of implementing specific lean practices, that work can be most impactful. In sum, there is clearly scope, and some significant encouragement because of the secondary data sets that can be used in such studies, to better consider and combine macro-level factors in OM research.

Sustainability

There is one area where OM is increasingly engaged with its socio-political context: the study of responses to the existential concerns triggered by climate change and other environmental degradation (Angell and Klassen 1999; Kleindorfer et al. 2005). Drake and Spinler (2013) present the question of pollutant emissions in queuing terms:

> If the average arrival rate of waste into an ecosystem exceeds the average rate at which that waste can be served by that ecosystem (i.e., removed from or assimilated by it), then waste will accumulate infinitely and that ecosystem is unstable; that is, the level of emissions being injected into the system is unsustainable. Therefore, evaluating ecosystem stability with respect to waste emissions requires an understanding of a pollutant's arrival rate into the system and the rates at which the pollutant can be removed from and assimilated by the system.
>
> (p. 692)

We have not addressed the topic so far, not because it is unimportant (indeed it is probably *the most important* topic) but rather because it is so difficult to categorize from a narrow disciplinary perspective.[13] Studies of the link between environmental and operations performance (Jiménez and Lorente 2001) continue to multiply, with interest in 'green' products and processes, reducing waste and CO_2 emissions, recycling and reverse logistics or closed-loop supply chains, etc. As Walker et al. (2014) note in the introduction to their IJOPM Special Issue, sustainable OM research covers "product design and eco-design, adoption of environmental and social standards, process improvement and lean operations, purchasing, supply chain management (SCM), logistics including recycling and closed-loop systems, performance measurement and risk management". Moreover, as the Walker et al. review also highlights, sustainability is an increasingly diffuse concept requiring consideration of environmental, ethical and economic – the so-called 'triple bottom line' (TBL) – objectives. The 17 United Nations Sustainable Development Goals provide an even more ambitious (diffuse?) backdrop for this conversation, leading some (e.g., Wiengarten et al. 2017) to explicitly frame it through a complexity lens. Significant OM-related questions arise therefore: do such goals trade-off against one another? Recent work suggests meaningful responses to the tensions inherent in the TBL necessitates potentially radical innovations but evidence of these in practice remains limited (Pagell and Shevchenko 2014). Equally, just as the field is trying to better incorporate people into its analyses, what are the implications of anthropocentric ethical considerations, providing moral standing to nonhuman entities including animals, plants and ecosystems? Such questions lead us back to the earlier challenge regarding connection to practice. Just because many OM scholars are interested in the topic, OM's actual value to the field of sustainability will likely hinge on connecting macro concerns with micro insights regarding actual changes to actual firms' actual operations (Chan et al. 2016). At its core the sustainability challenge is about confronting managers with 'temporal' tensions; how to satisfy current requirements without compromising future needs.

Time

OM could be viewed as the most 'temporal' of the management disciplines. It is the objective foundation for core concepts like process and flow (together with takt time, cycle time, learning curve, clock speed, scheduling, forecasting, used as a metric to compare the efficiency of different analytical heuristics, etc.) and subjectively understood in the world of queueing and customer service. And yet, more profound reflections on the nature of time and temporality are largely absent (cf. Ancona et al. 2001). In this text discussions of 'past', 'present' and 'future' have been used (uncritically) as generally accepted categorizations; in part as a way of establishing a wider perspective, helping to both understand where a discipline comes from, gets its sense of identity and traditions whilst also addressing how contemporary practices have developed and exploring potential and possible futures. What does it mean for OM when, from a scientific perspective,[14] clock time is acknowledged as an abstraction (Rovelli 2011)? What are the differences between clock time and event time? What does it mean for sequence-based process constructs – coding narrative data into sequences of coded events (Pentland 1999) – if the idea of an irreversible sequence of events, with a beginning and an end, moving in one direction is misleading? What if a more cyclical representation holds instead, whereby events are not immutable elements of causal chains but "states of being" that are forever present, stable and unchanging? Consider the widely cited 'banana time' example (Roy 2017). After observing a small group he noted how, with their work days spent doing simple repetitive boring tasks, critical "times" were actually the breaks in the daily routine, typically organized around food or drink: coffee time, peach time, fish time, lunch time, banana time, etc. Each was an opportunity for some kind of ritualized group interaction.

> Approximately an hour after peach time came banana time. Sammy, again, brought in one banana, but, before he could eat it, Ike would snatch it out of Sammy's lunch box, yell "banana time," and gulp down the banana. Sammy never got to eat his banana, but each day the group got to enjoy Sammy's complaints and denunciations.
>
> (Roy 2017, originally 1958)

Banana time has been interpreted in multiple ways. Breaks can be readily captured on a linear process map showing alternating work and social activities, but an understanding of socially constructed time further highlights the *need* for groups (especially in repetitive task environments) to create diversions that break up monotonous work. And what about time culture? The terms polychronic and monochronic, introduced by Hall (1959), remain under-explored in OM. Monochronic cultures typically engage in one activity at a time whereas polychronic cultures engage in several activities simultaneously, with consequent impact on individual and group behaviour. If time is viewed as cyclical for example, one will be much less affected by any one incident. This also raises profound issues when we consider what happens as we move across temporal cultures (Gray and Massimino 2014) – as Hall notes, what happens when a German manager wonders why a French employee has not finished one task on time, just as the employee wonders how his manager can be so single-task focused?

What has stopped OM from thinking more deeply about time? Perhaps it is a question of methodology – longitudinal work, especially panel data type approaches, has been a relatively small part of the OM canon – and measuring complex temporal phenomena was until relatively recently a significant undertaking, especially if looking for increasingly/decreasingly nonlinear patterns. Or perhaps, as Ancona et al. (2001) point out with reference to management research more broadly, researcher 'time' is itself socially constructed (e.g., PhD funding, tenure track, grant funding, etc.) and poorly suited for a focus on, especially long periods of, time. To help promote a temporal research agenda, they also develop a categorization that should be useful for OM scholars. They identify three distinct, but interconnecting, time categories and a range of variables that fit within them: time conception, mapping activities to time and actors relating to time (see Table 7.1).

Returning to our collage theme once again, the overlaps between the categories are also interesting. For example, process mapping, using defined activity beginnings and durations is also mapping time conceptions (i.e., clock time) and is conceptually distinct from a process map of, say, a product development process, which is likely using event time. If we use subjective time, as we might with service blueprinting, each actor will have her own map. More pragmatically, consider the Andon cord on an assembly line. Workers are supposed to pull the cord (or push the button) to stop the line if they notice a defect. Supervisors, etc.

Table 7.1 Time categories and subcategories with indicative variables

Category	Subcategory	Indicative Variables
Time conception	Types of time	Linear time, uniform time, cyclical time, subjective time, event time
	Socially constructed time	Work organization (normal hours, work time, family time), celebrations, etc.
Mapping activities to time	Single activity mapping	Schedule, completion, duration
	Repeated activity mapping	Cycle time, frequency, Ca, Cs
	Single activity transformation mapping	Project life cycle, gates, deadline behaviour, skills development
	Multiple activity mapping	Allocation of time resource, process synchronization, audit cycles
	Comparison and meshing of activity	Entrainment, *heijunka*, symmetry
Actors relating to time	Temporal perception	Experience of time passing, duration
	Temporal personality	Temporal orientation, temporal style

Source: Adapted from Ancona et al. 2001.

then arrive to support the worker and (hopefully) rectify the problem. From a time perspective, pulling the cord is actually a mechanism for switching from one-time mode to another, from linear work with clear time targets to a more cyclical, collaborative approach focused on events and resolution.

A deeper engagement with time and temporality creates multiple prospects for uncovering new perspectives, or allow for a re-appraisal of previously established insights. This might be exploring the entrainment of linear operations with financial reporting cycles (e.g., inventory holding and sales promotions patterns) or the interactions of different time horizons between shiftwork supervisors, divisional accountants and board directors or the characteristics of management decision and accountability in pre-project activities or the nature of 'banana time' in agile continuous software delivery processes, etc. Or consider a time-based interpretation of the Buurtzorg ("Neighborhood Care") senior care model. Founded in the Netherlands in 2006 with one team of 4 nurses, by 2018 they had 870 teams and 10,000 nurses and the approach was being piloted in many other countries. It is implemented via the use of self-managed teams who determine the schedule and task mix necessary to provide care for groups of 50 to 60 clients. This unusual emphasis on care givers controlling their own schedules is intrinsic to their carer-centric approach, as is the front-loading of care provision for clients, recognizing both the objective value of early support to create greater independence and community connection and subjective value of initial event experience. In one of the few OM studies to consider temporal orientation as a lens, Voss and Blackmon (1998), using data from a manufacturing strategy study that gathered data from 600 companies in 20 countries, found strong contrasts between Japan and 'the West' to be consistent with regional differences in strategic time orientation. Clearly cultural and organizational time perspectives (e.g., Toyota and their long-term plans) have a significant impact on questions of continuous improvement but scholars interested in Gemba could consider eschewing a focus on chronological time, choosing instead to focus on socio-spatial context – pathways, names, ritual, etc. Economic and psychological research acknowledges that individuals and organizations, when faced with an intertemporal choice, typically focus on the short term at the expense of the long term (Laverty 1996; Marginson et al. 2014; Marginson and McAulay 2008). Dealing with such intertemporal problems is perhaps the defining 'fact of life' for operational managers. Some actions satisfy long-run imperatives (e.g., continuous improvement, developing new products) but can harm short-term objectives (e.g., profit and liquidity targets, dividends, etc.). Returning to the earlier discussion of sustainability, this is an area replete with temporal paradox (Longoni and Cagliano 2018; Slawinski and Bansal 2015). Firms are able to reduce both greenhouse gas emissions and operating costs through energy efficiency, but this does little to address the fundamental challenge of fossil fuel energy. In other words, even well-intentioned short-term solutions can conceal deeper long-term systemic problems. Performance measurement can help but it raises important questions regarding appropriate balance of control? If profit-related measures, for example, become myopic, managers can select alternative measures that direct attention to the longer term. Do firms, like Toyota and Shell, that deliberately juxtapose short- and long-term aspects of an issue reveal a wider range of solutions than are available to firms that limit their time perspective?

Final thoughts

Concluding such a diverse state of the art review in a coherent fashion is an other almost impossible task, but there is one 'grand challenge' that brings together key themes. Psychological theory and methods (increasingly popular as part of BeOM) have been heavily criticized in recent years. Psychology has, as a result, been reflecting on the fundamental nature of the 'scientific' research process, challenging long-held assumptions about the nature of science such as transparency, openness and reproducibility. Within the management discipline there have been high-profile scandals (e.g., Lichtenthaler & Ernst 2012) that have led to calls for greater transparency and oversight. Of course, as always, context matters here. Refereed (top-tier) journal articles outputs have become, globally, the most important determinant of academic career success. "Publish or perish" ensures research productivity but may lead researchers to engage in questionable research practices (QRPs). In most cases (hopefully) this incentive structure does lead to misconduct such as fabricating data but this discussion does reconnect us with our art and artist metaphors, via the question of forgery. As the global art market flourishes (and art investments outperform the stock market, etc.) incentives for forgery ("art intended to deceive") increase and consequently, forgeries inevitably comprise a significant portion of the market. There is more demand for specific artists than there is supply.[15] Although exact numbers cannot be established, a former director of the NY Metropolitan Museum of Art has claimed that potentially 40% of the works at the Met could be forged! Interestingly, although the artistic impulse, like the division of labour, is an ancient one, through most of the history of art, artists have been anonymous. In both ancient Egypt and later in Rome, for example, sculptors and painters were paid artisans and credit only accrued to those who commissioned the work. Similarly, art in Western Europe in the Middle Ages primarily served as illustration (of history, religious devotion, etc.) and consequently, the identity of the artist was irrelevant. Authorship as a phenomenon probably first emerged in Ancient Greece, a society that both revered and analyzed artistic and aesthetic qualities. Consequently, there was a healthy market and competition among artists who signed their works to differentiate and assure quality. It was not until the Renaissance that European artists regularly began to identify their works and, with this process, market values began to rise and correspondingly, forgery rates rose as well. Ironically, it is the legendary Michelangelo who is also known for one of the first recorded instances of forgery. In 1496 he buried a sculpture (of Cupid, now lost) so it would appear older and hence more valuable.[16] In other words, forgery is an inevitable part of the art world and as that market has boomed, questions of authenticity and authentication have come increasingly to the fore. Scholarly QRPs typically fall short of this unethical behaviour[17] and for many qualms about outcome-reporting bias (e.g., null results are published less frequently than statistically significant results and therefore not available to other scholars as they undertake their related research) are easily lost in, what O'Boyle Jr et al. (2017) call the "Chrysalis Effect", the transformation from the caterpillar (initial results) to butterfly (journal article). There are many practices that *can* be questionable[18] – including 'presenting post hoc findings as a priori, "cherry picking" fit indices, and selectively deleting outliers for the purpose of achieving statistical significance' (O'Boyle Jr et al. 2017) – especially when the practices are either hidden or misreported.

Towards an open OM?

Open science is multi-faceted and includes elements – such as data sharing to improve reproducibility – that can seem both obvious and also be very difficult to implement, especially in a discipline like OM that often works with for-profit organizations seeking commercial confidentiality? We have already discussed how important and yet difficult encouraging replication studies is but this is also a key part of open scholarship. Other aspects seem more straightforward, such as explicitly justifying statistical significance thresholds to allow for more trustworthy interpretations of research findings, but still require collective community action (e.g., all journal editors?). One powerful approach, yet to surface in OM, is the pre-registering of studies and analytical approaches so as to better distinguish between confirmatory and exploratory research. The purpose and benefits of open science also need to be very clear. Some argue that increased confidence in scholarship could reduce the science-practice gap but others, and personal experience, suggest this is unlikely to be a panacea for what is in many ways a very different question. Banks et al. (2018) summarize a range of more pragmatic benefits for scholarship, that have profound resonance with the challenges of OM. Open science can promote collaboration. The sharing of data (and digital object identifiers allow researchers to be assigned appropriate credit) facilitate greater communication between researchers with similar interests. It can also support meta-analytic reviews that are potentially more useful and effective. The separation and sharing of design protocols, measures and analytic scripts should also help to improve the rigour of research designs as well as reproducibility and replication rates and, as data sets, these shared resources can be cited to give researchers credit for their intellectual contributions. Ultimately although significant questions remain, especially in a discipline like OM that often works with for-profit organizations seeking commercial confidentiality, it seems highly likely that the challenge of open science will do as much to shape the future 'state of the art' in OM as any theoretical ambitions or empirical techniques or specific process, control, people, strategy or technology questions that arise in practice.

Postscript

I hope that this review has been an illuminating use of your time; that it helps convey the breadth and depth of a field that combines deep historical roots with extensive contemporary global scholarship. To conclude let me wish my current and future colleagues, whatever picture they choose to paint or whatever art emerges from their work all the very best with the process.

Notes

1 The city of Bath, where I work, is a UK World Heritage site, known globally for its hot springs, Roman-built baths (Aquae Sulis), beautiful Georgian architecture and Jane Austen.
2 A popular European style of architecture inspired by the designs of Venetian architect Andrea Palladio (1508–1580).
3 Sir Eduardo Luigi Paolozzi (7 March 1924–22 April 2005), widely considered to be one of the pioneers of pop art, was a Scottish sculptor and artist.
4 Roach (2005) notes that even the classic EOQ (Harris 1913) was derived (perhaps unconsciously, definitely without acknowledgment) by adapting Kelvin's Law – a heuristic used in power systems to establish the most economical cross-section of a conductor such that transmission line cost is minimized. Interestingly, the contemporary critique of both EOQ and Kelvin is also very similar; any policy determined by these laws will be undermined by restrictive assumptions regarding various dynamic system factors.
5 Repenning and Sterman (2002) for example, conclude from their SD modelling that the success of process improvement is predicated on the interaction between the physical structure of the workplace and attribution biases in determining who or what was responsible for poor performance.
6 Mea culpa! Lewis (2000) is probably a good (bad?) example of additional, ad-hoc, specifying from original theoretical perspectives.
7 Most OM researchers have adopted either the definition of mediation provided by Baron and Kenny (1986), the generative mechanism through which a focal exogenous independent variable is able to influence its dependent consequence, or Venkatraman (1989), the existence of a significant intervening mechanism between antecedent and consequent variables.

8 Styhre notes that in Japan, the employee could demonstrate her attachment to the collective through kaizen whereas in Sweden it was used to enable self-fulfilment and individual well-being.

9 Vargo and Lusch (2004, 2008) and others propose that the S-D logic comprises 10 premises: Service is the fundamental basis of exchange. Indirect exchange masks the fundamental basis of exchange. Goods are distribution mechanisms for service provision. Operant resources the fundamental source of competitive advantage. All economies are service economies. The customer is always a co-creator of value. The enterprise cannot deliver value, but only offer value propositions. A service-centered view is inherently customer-oriented and relational. All economic and social actors are resource integrators. Value is always uniquely and phenomenologically determined by the beneficiary.

10 Grounds are the (necessary but not sufficient, often empirical) starting point for a claim; warrants are the standards and principles applied to specifically connect grounds-claims; and backings establish the general foundation for the use of specific warrants.

11 Stock, J. H., & Watson, M. W. (2002). Has the business cycle changed and why? *NBER Macroeconomics Annual*, 17, 159–218.

12 These often rely on self-reported measures such as "Our customers often change their order over the month" (Wong et al. 2011).

13 It also emerged as a topic alongside the supply chain turn in OM and hence many of the key works are a little out of scope (e.g., Guide and Van Wassenhove 2009).

14 The theory of relativity concludes that an individuals' measure of time is contingent on location and movement (e.g., Rovelli 2011). For a fantastic recent review, of what he calls the "spiderweb of time", read Carlo Rovelli's *Order of Time* (2017, Allen Lane).

15 Conversely of course, for elite journals there is more supply than demand.

16 Michelangelo sold it to a Cardinal Riario who, when he discovered it was artificially aged, actually allowed Michelangelo to keep his percentage as he was so impressed with the work (he demanded a refund from the dealer). Ultimately his forgery only added to his celebrity.

17 It should be noted however, as the Michelangelo story suggests, that ethical boundaries are not always that clear cut. There will always be a demand for copies of masterpieces, whether regarded as fakes or not, and the copying of masterpieces has long been regarded as a form of apprenticeship.

18 Exploratory data analysis can be invaluable and outliers should be examined and, at times, dropped from further analysis (Aguinis et al. 2013).

References

Aguinis, H., Gottfredson, R. K., & Joo, H. (2013). Best-practice recommendations for defining, identifying, and handling outliers. *Organizational Research Methods*, 16(2), 270–301.

Anand, G., & Gray, J. V. (2017). Strategy and organization research in operations management. *Journal of Operations Management*, 53, 1–8.

Ancona, D. G., Goodman, P. S., Lawrence, B. S., & Tushman, M. L. (2001). Time: A new research lens. *Academy of Management Review*, 26(4), 645–663.

Ancona, D. G., Okhuysen, G. A., & Perlow, L. A. (2001). Taking time to integrate temporal research. *The Academy of Management Review*, 26, 512–529.

Angell, L. C., & Klassen, R. D. (1999). Integrating environmental issues into the mainstream: An agenda for research in operations management. *Journal of Operations Management*, 17(5), 575–598.

Azadegan, A., Patel, P. C., Zangoueinezhad, A., & Linderman, K. (2013). The effect of environmental complexity and environmental dynamism on lean practices. *Journal of Operations Management*, 31(4), 193–212.

Banks, G. C., Field, J. G., Oswald, F. L., O'Boyle, E. H., Landis, R. S., Rupp, D. E., & Rogelberg, S. G. (2018). Answers to 18 questions about open science practices. *Journal of Business and Psychology*, 1–14.

Baron, R. M., & Kenny, D. A. (1986). The moderator–mediator variable distinction in social psychological research: Conceptual, strategic, and statistical considerations. *Journal of Personality and Social Psychology*, 51(6), 1173.

Boer, H., Holweg, M., Kilduff, M., Pagell, M., Schmenner, R., & Voss, C. (2015). Making a meaningful contribution to theory. *International Journal of Operations & Production Management*, 35(9), 1231–1252.

Bromiley, P., & Rau, D. (2016). Operations management and the resource based view: Another view. *Journal of Operations Management*, 41, 95–106.

Chan, T. Y., Wong, C. W., Lai, K. H., Lun, V. Y., Ng, C. T., & Ngai, E. W. (2016). Green service: Construct development and measurement validation. *Production and Operations Management*, 25(3), 432–457.

Corvellec, H., & Hultman, J. (2014). Managing the politics of value propositions. *Marketing Theory*, 14(4), 355–375.

Delbridge, R., & Fiss, P. C. (2013). Editors' comments: Styles of theorizing and the social organization of knowledge. *Academy of Management Review*, 38, 325–331.

Drake, D. F., & Spinler, S. (2013). OM forum: Sustainable operations management: An enduring stream or a passing fancy? *Manufacturing & Service Operations Management*, 15(4), 689–700.

Field, J. M., Victorino, L., Buell, R. W., Dixon, M. J., Meyer Goldstein, S., Menor, L. J., & Zhang, J. J. (2018). Service operations: What's next? *Journal of Service Management*, 29(1), 55–97.

Frohlich, M. T., & Dixon, J. R. (2006). Reflections on replication in OM research and this special issue. *Journal of Operations Management*, 6(24), 865–867.

Gavronski, I., Klassen, R. D., Johnson, P. F., & Naranjo, F. (2018). Management temporal orientation: Linking operational investment to corporate social responsibility. *Academy of Management Proceedings*, 2018(1), 18376. Briarcliff Manor, NY 10510: Academy of Management, 2018.

Goldstein, S. M. (2003). Employee development: An examination of service strategy in a high-contact service environment. *Production and Operations Management*, 12(2), 186–203.

Gray, J. V., & Massimino, B. (2014). The effect of language differences and national culture on operational process compliance. *Production and Operations Management*, 23(6), 1042–1056.

Guide Jr, V. D. R., & Ketokivi, M. (2015). Notes from the Editors: Redefining some methodological criteria for the journal⋆. *Journal of Operations Management*, 37(1), v–viii.

Guide, V. D. R., & Van Wassenhove, L. N. (2009). The evolution of closed-loop supply chain research. *Operations Research*, 57(1), 10–18.

Hall, E. (1959). *The Silent Language*. Garden City, NY: Doubleday.

Hausman, W. H., Lee, H. L., & Subramanian, U. (2013). The impact of logistics performance on trade. *Production and Operations Management*, 22(2), 236–252.

Hendricks, K. B., & Singhal, V. R. (2003). The effect of supply chain glitches on shareholder wealth. *Journal of operations Management*, 21(5), 501–522.

Holmström, J., Ketokivi, M., & Hameri, A. P. (2009). Bridging practice and theory: a design science approach. *Decision Sciences*, 40(1), 65–87.

Jiménez, J., & Lorente, J. J. (2001). Environmental performance as an operations objective. International *Journal of Operations & Production Management*, 21(12), 1553–1572.

Kaplan, A. (1964). *The conduct of inquiry*. Chandler, Scranton. Pa.

Karmarkar, U. (2015). OM forum: The service and information economy: Research opportunities. *Manufacturing & Service Operations Management*, 17(2), 136–141.

Kenworthy, T., & Balakrishnan, J. (2016). Theory usage in empirical operations management research: A review and discussion. *Management Decision*, 54(10), 2413–2432.

Ketokivi, M. (2006). Elaborating the contingency theory of organizations: The case of manufacturing flexibility strategies. *Production and Operations Management*, 15(2), 215–228.

Ketokivi, M., Mantere, S., & Cornelissen, J. (2017). Reasoning by analogy and the progress of theory. *Academy of Management Review*, 42(4).

Kleindorfer, P. R., Singhal, K., & Van Wassenhove, L. N. (2005). Sustainable operations management. *Production and Operations Management*, 14(4), 482–492.

Kuhn, T. (1962). *The structure of scientific revolutions*. Chicago Univ. Press, Chicago.

Laverty, K. J. (1996). Economic "short-termism": The debate, the unresolved issues, and the implications for management practice and research. *Academy of Management Review*, 21(3), 825–860.

Lee Park, C., & Paiva, E. L. (2018). How do national cultures impact the operations strategy process? *International Journal of Operations & Production Management*.

Lewis, M. A. (2000). Lean production and sustainable competitive advantage. *International Journal of Operations & Production Management*, 20(8), 959–978.

Lichtenthaler, U., & Ernst, H. (2012). RETRACTED: Integrated knowledge exploitation: The complementarity of product development and technology licensing. *Strategic Management Journal*, 33(5), 513–534.

Longoni, A., & Cagliano, R. (2018). Sustainable innovativeness and the triple bottom line: The role of organizational time perspective. *Journal of Business Ethics*, 151(4), 1097–1120.

Lovejoy, W. S. (1998). Integrated operations: A proposal for operations management teaching and research. *Production and Operations Management*, 7(2), 106–124.

MacCarthy, B. L., Lewis, M., Voss, C., & Narasimhan, R. (2013). The same old methodologies? Perspectives on OM research in the post-lean age. *International Journal of Operations & Production Management*, 33(7), 934–956.

Malhotra, M. K., Singhal, C., Shang, G., & Ployhart, R. E. (2014). A critical evaluation of alternative methods and paradigms for conducting mediation analysis in operations management research. *Journal of Operations Management*, 32(4), 127–137.

Marginson, D., & McAulay, L. (2008). Exploring the debate on short-termism: A theoretical and empirical analysis. *Strategic Management Journal*, 29(3), 273–292.

Marginson, D., McAulay, L., Roush, M., & van Zijl, T. (2014). Examining a positive psychological role for performance measures. *Management Accounting Research*, 25(1), 63–75.

Meredith, J. R., Krajewski, L., Hill, A. V., & Handfield, R. B. (2002). 20th anniversary of JOM: An editorial retrospective and prospective. *Journal of Management*, 22(2), 119–150.

Meredith, J. R., & Pilkington, A. (2018). Assessing the exchange of knowledge between operations management and other fields: Some challenges and opportunities. *Journal of Operations Management*, 60, 47–53.

Narasimhan, R. (2014). Theory development in operations management: Extending the frontiers of a mature discipline via qualitative research. *Decision Sciences*, 45(2), 209–227.

Nosek, B. A., Alter, G., Banks, G. C., Borsboom, D., Bowman, S. D., Breckler, S. J., & Contestabile, M. (2015). Promoting an open research culture. *Science*, 348(6242), 1422–1425.

O'Boyle Jr, E. H., Banks, G. C., & Gonzalez-Mulé, E. (2017). The chrysalis effect: How ugly initial results metamorphosize into beautiful articles. *Journal of Management*, 43(2), 376–399.

Pagell, M., & Shevchenko, A. (2014). Why research in sustainable supply chain management should have no future. *Journal of Supply Chain Management*, 50(1), 44–55.

Pentland, B. T. (1999). Building process theory with narrative: From description to explanation. *Academy of Management Review*, 24, 711–724.

Perlow, L. A. (1999). The time famine: Toward a sociology of work time. *Administrative Science Quarterly*, 44(1), 57–81.

Perrow, C. (2011). *Normal Accidents: Living with High Risk Technologies* (Updated ed.). Princeton, NJ: Princeton University Press.

Repenning, N. P. (2001). Understanding firefighting in new product development. *Journal of Product Innovation Management*, 18(5), 285–300.

Repenning, N. P., & Sterman, J. D. (2002). Capability traps and self-confirming attribution errors in the dynamics of process improvement. *Administrative Science Quarterly*, 47(2), 265–295.

Roach, B. (2005). Origin of the economic order quantity formula: Transcription or transformation? *Management Decision*, 43(9), 1262–1268.

Rovelli, C. (2011). Forget time. *Foundations of Physics*, 41(9), 1475.

Roy, D. F. (2017). "Banana time" job satisfaction and informal interaction. In *The Anthropology of Organisations* (pp. 31–41). Abingdon, UK: Routledge.

Rungtusanatham, M. J., Choi, T. Y., Hollingworth, D. G., Wu, Z., & Forza, C. (2003). Survey research in operations management: Historical analyses. *Journal of Operations Management*, 21(4), 475–488.

Sampson, S. E., & Froehle, C. M. (2006). Foundations and implications of a proposed unified services theory. *Production and Operations Management*, 15(2), 329–343.

Schmenner, R. W., & Swink, M. L. (1998). On theory in operations management. *Journal of Operations Management*, 17(1), 97–113.

Schmenner, R. W., Van Wassenhove, L., Ketokivi, M., Heyl, J., & Lusch, R. F. (2009). Too much theory, not enough understanding. *Journal of Operations Management*, 27(5), 339–343.

Schon, D. A. (1983). *The reflective practitioner: How professionals think in action*. New York: Basic Books.

Schroeder, R. G., Bates, K. A., & Junttila, M. A. (2002). A resource-based view of manufacturing strategy and the relationship to manufacturing performance. *Strategic Management Journal*, 23, 2105–2117.

Shah, R., & Ward, P. T. (2003). Lean manufacturing: context, practice bundles, and performance. *Journal of Operations Management*, 21(2), 129–149.

Shalley, C. E., & Gilson, L. L. (2017). Creativity and the management of technology: Balancing creativity and standardization. *Production and Operations Management*, 26(4), 605–616.

Slawinski, N., & Bansal, P. (2015). Short on time: Intertemporal tensions in business sustainability. *Organization Science*, 26(2), 531–549.

Soltani, E., Ahmed, P. K., Ying Liao, Y., & Anosike, P. U. (2014). Qualitative middle-range research in operations management: The need for theory-driven empirical inquiry. *International Journal of Operations & Production Management*, 34(8), 1003–1027.

Sousa, R., & Voss, C. A. (2008). Contingency research in operations management practices. *Journal of Operations Management*, 26(6), 697–713.

Styhre, A. (2001). Kaizen, ethics, and care of the operations: Management after empowerment. *Journal of Management Studies*, 38(6), 795–810.

Toulmin, S. E. (2003). *The uses of argument*. Cambridge University Press.

Van Driel, H., & Dolfsma, W. (2009). Path dependence, initial conditions, and routines in organizations: The Toyota production system re-examined. *Journal of Organizational Change Management*, 22(1), 49–72.

Vargo, S. L., & Lusch, R. F. (2004). Evolving to a new dominant logic for marketing. *Journal of Marketing*, 68 (January), 1–17.

Vargo, S. L., & Lusch, R. F. (2008). Service-dominant logic: Continuing the evolution. *Journal of the Academy of Marketing Science*, 36 (Spring), 1–10.

Venkatesh, V., Bala, H., & Sykes, T. A. (2010). Impacts of information and communication technology implementations on employees' jobs in service organizations in India: A multi-method longitudinal field study. *Production and Operations Management*, 19(5), 591–613.

Venkatraman, N. (1989). The concept of fit in strategy research: Toward verbal and statistical correspondence. *Academy of Management Review*, 14(3), 423–444.

Victorino, L., Field, J. M., Buell, R. W., Dixon, M. J., Goldstein, S. M., Menor, L. J., Pullman, M. E., Roth, A. V., Secchi, E., & Zhang, J. J. (2018). Service operations: What have we learned? *Journal of Service Management*, 29(1), 39–54.

Voss, C., & Blackmon, K. (1998). Differences in manufacturing strategy decisions between Japanese and Western manufacturing plants: The role of strategic time orientation. *Journal of Operations Management*, 16(2–3), 147–158.

Wacker, J. G. (2004). A theory of formal conceptual definitions: Developing theory-building measurement instruments. *Journal of Operations Management*, 22(6), 629–650.

Walker, P. H., Seuring, P. S., Sarkis, P. J., & Klassen, P. R. (2014). Sustainable operations management: recent trends and future directions. *International Journal of Operations & Production Management*, 34(5).

Ward, P. T., & Duray, R. (2000). Manufacturing strategy in context: Environment, competitive strategy and manufacturing strategy. *Journal of Operations Management*, 18(2), 123–138.

Ward, P. T., Duray, R., Leong, G. K., & Sum, C. C. (1995). Business environment, operations strategy, and performance: an empirical study of Singapore manufacturers. *Journal of Operations Management*, 13(2), 99–115.

Wiengarten, F., Ahmed, M. U., Longoni, A., Pagell, M., & Fynes, B. (2017). Complexity and the triple bottom line: An information-processing perspective. *International Journal of Operations & Production Management*, 37(9), 1142–1163.

Wolf, F. G. (2001). Operationalizing and testing normal accident theory in petrochemical plants and refineries. *Production and Operations Management*, 10(3), 292–305.

Wong, C. Y., Boon-Itt, S., & Wong, C. W. (2011). The contingency effects of environmental uncertainty on the relationship between supply chain integration and operational performance. *Journal of Operations Management*, 29(6), 604–615.

Index

Note: Page numbers in *italic* indicate a figure. Page numbers in **bold** indicate a table. Page numbers followed by an "n" denote a note on the corresponding page.

For Product Safety Concerns and Information please contact our EU
representative GPSR@taylorandfrancis.com
Taylor & Francis Verlag GmbH, Kaufingerstraße 24, 80331 München, Germany